LOSING YOU,
FINDING ME

KAY BACKHOUSE

First Edition published 2023 by
2QT Limited (Publishing) Stockport, UK United Kingdom

The author has her own website: www.kaybackhouse.com

Cover Design by Charlotte Mouncey www.bookstyle.co.uk

Printed in Great Britain by Ingram Sparks

A CIP catalogue record for this book is available from the British Library
ISBN - 978-1-914083-93-8

For Syd, from my heart to yours

CONTENTS

PART THREE
REMEMBERING

INTRODUCTION

Every story is us.
Rumi

I almost didn't write this book.

It was a mountain I was sure I could not and would not climb.

Yet here we are.

I dreamt of writing a book for what felt like my entire life, but the truth was I never felt good enough; I didn't think I had the right to claim I was a writer. I didn't go to university, nor did I attend a single writing class; I have no formal qualifications – and who was I to think I was so special, anyway? The truth is, I was suffering from a terrible case of imposter syndrome, and I was mired in old beliefs that I wasn't worthy, let alone capable. But no matter how much of an imposter I felt, I just couldn't get the image of my finished book, all bound and beautiful, out of my head. It kept nudging me, quietly whispering to me.

But what should I write about? I had no idea. I just knew I was compelled to write, and I had an absolute knowing that one day something would happen in my life that would be worth writing about. I just had to be patient, stay aware and wait for the right time. Then in 2014 the story I was going to tell became clear. I had a story, something I knew I would want to share in the years to come. The seeds of intention were sown, but it would be over seven years before my pen would touch the paper.

For as long as I can remember, I have been obsessed with words in all their forms. It's as if they have a life force of their own. I echo the words of the late, great poet Maya Angelou when she said that 'words are things'. I truly believe that words carry their own essence and energy which has the capability to move and affect the person it reaches in any exchange or medium.

Henry David Thoreau put it beautifully when he wrote these exquisite words in his book *Walden*.

A written word is the choicest of relics. It is something at once more intimate with us and more universal than any other work of art. It is the work of art nearest to life itself. It may be translated into every language, and not only be read but actually breathed from human lips;— not represented on canvas or marble only but be carved out of the breath of life itself.

My fascination with words and the human psyche grew as I entered my early teenage years. I would often wonder: why do we do the things we do? How do we express how we are feeling inside using language? How do the words we use affect others?

I have come to know that the way I process literature

and the world around me in general is and always has been at a deeper level than most. I find it difficult to stay in the shallows, chattering with the minnows – I am much more comfortable wading into the deep, murky waters with the whales. On the one hand, this trait I possess has brought so much joy into my life, acted out in the deep relationships I have forged with those closest to me. But on the other, it has caused me to suffer when my intensity has been misunderstood by others. At times throughout my life, I have been considered too full-on, too blunt, too opinionated, too righteous, too much to handle, and my inability to tolerate small talk and superficiality has pushed me, at times, to retreat from society. In every one of those difficult parts of my life, it has been literature, and my love for it, that has saved me. As my Gran used to say, 'reading keeps the demons away'.

In my early years, the first person that nurtured my love affair with all things written and spoken was my beautiful mum. It was in seeing her own love for literature – like the way she would smell the pages of her books as if she were inhaling a fresh bunch of flowers, or how she insisted no one touch her brand new magazines until she had touched them first – that really had me captivated. Watching her devour a book like a last meal was like nothing I had seen before, and I mirrored this behaviour from what seemed like the womb.

As a young girl, I could often be found reading my stack of Enid Blyton, Judy Blume, and Beatrix Potter books, escaping into the pages of the 'Famous Five' and their amazing adventures. I excelled in English at school. It was the only lesson on the timetable I genuinely looked forward to, and it would ease the pain of being in a place where I never felt completely myself. Like most children, I found school a difficult place – not just because of the enormity of the physical place, or the overstimulation I would often experience, but mainly driven by the fact that the archaic education system expects every child to excel in every subject. For a highly sensitive person (a trait a minority of the population carry), a perfectionist, and a people-pleaser, this was truly exhausting and, in many ways, soul-destroying. There's a great saying: 'Everybody is a genius. But if you judge a fish by its ability to climb a tree, it will live its whole life believing that it's stupid.'

This so-called 'modern' education system left me believing I was stupid and, often, a failure. I would ask myself, 'Why aren't I a straight-A student like the others?' I believed my grades defined who I was and my value in the world. I was sure that I wasn't intelligent and was ultimately not 'good enough' unless I was achieving straight As. It seemed to me that it was the only marker of success. The truth was, I was the fish, and I was trying desperately to climb the tree. No one encouraged me to swim in the water.

The education system hasn't changed in any significant way since I attended primary school over thirty years ago. Children are still taught that success is measured by their ability to memorise and repeat information, follow rules and instructions set by others, and to 'be yourself (just not like that!)'. Success is rarely measured by the ability to think for yourself.

In his book Freedom from the Known, J Krishnamurti, put it well when he said:

> *The school should help its young people to discover their vocations and responsibilities, and not merely cram their mind with facts and technical knowledge; it should be the soil in which they can grow without fear, happily and integrally.*

And, just like my own experience, we now have a huge portion of the general population believing they are not intelligent enough and will do anything that anyone in authority tells them to do without question – even if their gut instinct tells them the opposite.

The irony is that many of us spend much of our lives searching for the very thing we already knew when we were young. We should've trusted our instincts. There is a light inside each and every one of us – and it was there all along, showing us the way, but that light slowly became dimmed by the pressure and influence of those around us and their need for us to 'fit in' to a 'one size fits all' society.

We were never truly shown what we need to thrive in life – how to be in nature, for example, or how *feeling* good is so much more important than *looking* good. We weren't taught that the real mark of success is to build a life full of love, purpose, peace, and contentment, or that to be truly happy we must express ourselves authentically, rather than living a life based on what other people want or need. Instead, we were programmed to compete and win at all costs. We were taught to chase money, status and titles, and to live to excess. We were promised that this was the ticket to happiness. But the end result is quite the opposite: we have become unhappy, disenchanted and uninspired, and we are struggling to keep our heads above water. We have lost our inner compass and are wandering aimlessly, looking for our true north in all the wrong places.

As I entered my adolescent years, challenges I faced in my life quickly and unknowingly steered me away from my passions, and I, like so many others, became distracted and disillusioned. For the next twenty years of my life, I would barely pick up a book, let alone write anything down. I stopped being curious about life. I locked myself inside what I refer to as the 'invisible cage' and fell asleep to life. Then, in 2011, major events in my life triggered an awakening process that shook me to the core, and slowly I began to make my way back to myself. As if waking from amnesia, I slowly began to remember the child in me that I had ignored and left behind many years before – that frightened part of me that needed to be loved again.

This is a story about love, death, grief, hope, and self-discovery. How tragedy can force you into uncomfortable places but can be used as a catalyst to bring you back to your true self. Life, I have learnt, is difficult. Our egoic mind, in its relentless pursuit to convince us we are separate from all other human beings, will try to tell us that our suffering has only ever happened to us, but of course that's not the case at all;

you would be hard-pressed to find anyone who hasn't also suffered during their own life. I truly believe our strength can be found in sharing our stories. Using language as a way to feel understood helps us to garner the authentic connection with, and belonging to, our fellow human beings that we are all so desperately seeking.

This book has been my passion project, my labour of love. Not only that; it has quite literally kept me alive. I once heard it said that, 'keeping trauma a secret can result in higher death rates by cancer and disease' (attributed to James Pennebaker, University of Texas) – and I refuse to become another statistic. I made a promise to my brother to share our story and be his voice, and I will continue to honour his life in the only way I know how: by helping others.

I am here to remind you: **you are not alone**.

PART ONE

ASLEEP

CHAPTER ONE: NOVEMBER

Acceptance of the unacceptable is the greatest
source of grace in this world.
Eckhart Tolle

Friday 9th November 2018. I arrived outside the hospital at around 3.30 p.m. I had just returned from four days of training in Watford for a new job I had started just two weeks prior, and I was exhausted. My body didn't know which way was up, and my mind was shot. As I stepped out of the car, I felt the miserable English winter hit my face – God, I missed Australia. I made a dash across the street, skipping and jumping, trying to avoid the puddles while wrestling with my umbrella to stop it flipping inside out in the wind, cursing to myself along the way. As I hurried into the pedestrian tunnel, I started my customary motivational speech on how to survive yet another hospital visit. Hospital visits are not much fun. I am yet to meet a single person who enjoys them. For me, they seem to invoke a sense of fear in my psyche, somewhere deep down in the abyss where we all try to keep the hard stuff locked away. Hospitals can be at best a place of comfort and recovery, and at the very worst a place of pain, suffering and death. My experience of hospital visits has usually been the latter, and they have always felt like an emotional assault on both my mind and body.

In 2006 my dad almost died. I remember it clear as day. It was an icy afternoon in February, a Saturday, and I was at home. My husband, Rick, was at the local football ground only five hundred metres away from our home, watching our boys, Louis and Taylor. They were just six and four at the time, so it wasn't so much a football match, more like a game of 'chase the football around a muddy field with the rest of the snotty-nosed kids like an obsessed swarm of bees'. Unbelievably frustrating to watch, and the reason why I wasn't there. Mother of the Year Award – I know. As I sat down in front of the TV with my cup of tea, the phone rang. It was my brother Dylan. It wasn't unusual for him to call on a weekend, so I wasn't particularly alarmed. That soon changed when I heard his voice.

'Come to Mum and Dad's now. It's Dad. He's come off his bike. Quick as you can.'

That was all he said in between tears. Dylan doesn't cry often, so when he does, I know it's bad. When I arrived, the ambulance had already taken my dad to the hospital. I listened intently as Dylan explained what had happened, and I felt my fear rising. My dad had fallen from his mountain bike on an icy downhill slope, in the middle of nowhere, and knocked himself unconscious. It came to light later that as he fell, the handlebar had turned 180 degrees and slammed straight into his torso. He was bleeding internally from a ruptured spleen, but no one knew. As we stepped into resus, I was faced with the very real possibility that my dad might die. It was the first time I had faced his mortality. To me,

Dad was invincible, born with a superpower that seemed to allow him to overcome any challenge put in front of him. Now here he was, weak as a kitten, his skin shiny and ashen, about to undergo life-saving surgery. As I clutched his cold hands, I said goodbye and told him how much I loved him. I was trying my hardest to stop every stitch of emotion from coming undone.

It's common knowledge in the medical arena that in most circumstances you have approximately twenty minutes with a spleen in that state, and without medical intervention, before you die. He had survived almost two hours. Unbelievably, and to the amazement of the surgeons, he walked out of that hospital unaided four days later. What we witnessed that day was a miracle.

Fast forward to 9th November 2018, and my faith in miracles was beginning to waver. As I quickly made my way down the familiar rabbit warren of corridors down to the acute assessment unit, I thought about how much I couldn't wait to see my little brother, Syd. He had been admitted to the local hospital three weeks earlier after a complication with his cancer – a cancer he had been fighting for over seven years. His cancer had been defined as 'terminal' in 2013, but he was defying all the odds.

'Here she is!' my mum shouted, greeting me like I was the most famous person in the world, as she often did – and I secretly loved it. I had been away for only a few days, but it felt like a year. I embraced my mum and dad before making my way over to my brother. He was sitting upright in bed, wearing his favourite blue T-shirt. It was slightly raised where his tumour pushed through from his chest. He looked tired. I knew he was still trying to process the past few weeks. His cancer had caused a serious complication, resulting in what is known as an adrenal crisis: the level of sodium in his body had become so dangerously low that he was just moments from death right in front of me. An emergency shot of steroids administered at the last moment saved his life. It was a traumatising experience for all of us, but especially for him. Physically it had been harrowing, but mentally it had been felt much more deeply. It seemed to unlock a chasm of emotions which had been buried deep in his soul for most of his adult life. And these emotions didn't just pour out; they came rushing out in all directions like uncontrollable white-water rapids, and he was struggling to stay afloat. More on this later.

'Here you go. Thought you'd fancy some of these,' I said, smiling, passing him a packet of Haribo and some Lindt chocolates. His eyes lit up; they were his favourite.

'Has Dr P been in yet?' I asked. My default mode whenever I arrived at the hospital was to find out what was going on and find solutions. It's always been part of who I am. I get stuff done, and it makes me feel productive in helpless situations. I understood a lot of the medical terminology and I knew how hospitals worked. I knew where to go and who to ask for. However, this also has its downsides. There's nowhere to hide. You end up knowing far more than you want to. Today was one of those moments, and I just hadn't seen it coming.

'Nah, he hasn't been in yet,' he said, his eyes rolling.

I gave his hand a squeeze, threw him a comforting glance and left the room to hunt down Dr P. As I headed out into the corridor, the nurses' station was buzzing with activity. I was reluctant to interrupt, but I grabbed the nearest nurse and asked to see Dr P. She explained he was on the ward, and she would take me to him. This was fantastic news and a wonderful stroke of luck.

'Hi! So good to see you again,' I said, shaking Dr P's hand for what felt like the thousandth time. We had become what I would call 'professional friends'. We could email him direct-ly and call him on his mobile. Syd would joke that it was one of the benefits of being terminally ill, having your specialists on speed dial. Dr P was Syd's endocrinologist, aka 'the hor-mone guy'. Knowing what I know now, I would argue that endocrinology is one of the most complex specialties known to humankind. In my brother's case, Dr P was given the im-possible task of understanding not only a cancer that only appeared in one in five million of the population, but also the cascade of dangerous hormonal imbalances that came along with it. They were impossible to predict and hoodwinked him (and us) at every turn. The cancer was sneaky and clever. It became like a game of whack-a-mole – except this wasn't fun at all. Dr P had a decent sense of humour, which was a prerequisite for being involved with our family. There was a pace that had to be kept up with, and if you didn't keep that pace, you were often left on the sidelines. You could sense his genuine empathy for our family and the circumstances we found ourselves in. He would sometimes turn up on week-ends fully kitted out in his cycling gear on his way home, just to check on Syd's progress. Always popping his head in on his break between ward rounds and clinics. We trusted him.

'Have you got Syd's scan results through yet?' I asked eagerly.

'Oh, yeah – sorry, I thought you'd already been given the report?' he said.

I could tell he was swamped, so I didn't question his reply or push for more information; I was just pleased I could get my hands on the report. He printed it off and handed it to me in a way that made me feel like a colleague rather than his patient's sister. There was no explanation regarding the details in the report, and to be honest I didn't think anything of it at the time. Reading our own reports was how my brother and I rolled now. By this time, we had become experts in his cancer. We often knew more than the specialists did. I will never forget the time I emailed him asking how his appointment with the specialist had gone, a few years prior. He emailed back as quick as a flash to give me the details. When I asked him what the doctors were planning to do next, he proceeded to tell me how he had leant over his consultant's desk, turned the computer screen around and told him what was going to happen next. He had always been a straight talker, but his confidence hadn't always been this high; it had grown over time, and he had found his own voice. I smirked to myself as I read his email and felt a sense of sisterly pride filling up my insides.

So, with the scan report firmly in my hands, I trotted back to Room Six. The conversations were still flowing when I entered the room, so I drifted in unnoticed and plonked myself down in the chair by the window. I settled in with a strange sort of excitement, curious as always about what was happening in my brother's insides. I was even casually pondering in the back of my mind which bottle of wine I was going to pick up on the way home, completely unaware of the impending doom. It had been a long week, so I was ready to put my feet up. As I read the first paragraph, not much disturbed me other than I noted the tumour in my brother's chest had grown exponentially. It measured 15cm by 10cm and, according to the scan, had 'encased the sternum' – it sounded like something from a horror movie, slowly infiltrating his chest with its long tentacles. The mound on his chest had been staring up at him every single day for the past year and a half, so this wasn't a surprise. He had watched it grow, like some sick reminder of his disease that he couldn't escape. It was the first thing he saw in the morning and the last thing he saw at night. What followed in the next paragraph, however, blindsided me. As I continued to digest the pages, I could sense my body pump out a surge of adrenaline. A burning sensation rushed up and down my entire body; I felt sick to my stomach, but tried my hardest not to attract any attention. By this time, the voices in the room seemed to be getting further and further away from me, I was becoming light-headed, and the room seemed to be drifting away. I knew exactly what was happening: I was having a panic attack. It wasn't my first and it wouldn't be my last. The mind–body connection in full flow. My brain was working a million miles an hour. How was I going to tell my brother what was happening? How would I tell Rick and the boys? And worst of all, how would we tell his son? I can only liken it to those moments people talk about when they see their lives flash before them. I sat there unmoved, frozen in time.

His cancer had spread everywhere. It hadn't just taken a bus trip; it had jumped on a jumbo jet and travelled around the world – his world– in eighty days. It had spread to his liver, spine, lymph nodes, lungs, and bones. The only places it hadn't gone were his kidneys and bowel. I mean, it was impressive– I had to give him that.

I calmly placed the report on my chair and excused myself from the room. I don't have any memory of the moments that followed, other than I know I was breathing heavily, trying to put one foot in front of the other and desperately trying not to buckle under the mountain of tears I had trapped inside of me. After some time in the visitors' bathroom and as soon as I felt like some sort of equilibrium had returned, I made my way back to my brother's room.

His curious, beady eyes greeted me from behind his glasses as I walked back in. I could see he was scanning my face and body for answers. He knew something was up.

'Well, it's not good news,' I said, laughing – trying desperately to make light of the situation. We always tried to make light of his illness; it was the only way to survive the painful moments.

He replied, 'I knew it wasn't. I can read you like a book. Come on, then, let's have it.'

I sat back down and with my voice wavering slightly, I read the report aloud word for word. It felt like it was happening to someone else.

As I finished the final sentence, I glanced up at my parents. They were sitting down and holding each other's hands tenderly. I could see that they had sensed this coming. One thing I know for sure is that parents know things; no one knows how, but they do.

Why didn't I know? For the very first time, I questioned whether it was hope that had kept me going or whether I had been in denial for the past seven years. Had I been lying to myself? Was everyone else watching and thinking 'God, the poor cow, she's got no idea what's coming . . .' ?

He joked, 'C'mon, you have to admit – that's pretty impressive, isn't it?'

'Oh, yes . . . you've really outdone yourself this time,' I quipped sarcastically.

There was nothing more to say. A strange stillness blanketed the room. We all sat there sensing each other's fear like a herd of deer when they sense a predator approaching.

All I could think was *That's it. It's all over*. I had to accept the unacceptable.

CHAPTER TWO:
THE IRON MASK

Children are born innocent. Before they are
domesticated, they live in the moment,
love without fear, and don't even think
about the opinions of others.
Don Miguel Ruiz

For the first nine years of my life, I grew up in a small village, Clayton, just three miles from Bradford in the north of England. I had an incredibly happy childhood. We lived in a lovely home. I had a loving family, and truly there isn't anything I would change. Dad was a pattern-maker – sadly, a dying art form now– and worked extremely hard. In the words of John Lennon, he was a true 'working-class hero'. He left school at fifteen with zero qualifications and nothing behind him, financially or otherwise. Knowing what I know now about his childhood fills me with pride every day when I think of everything he has achieved in such difficult circumstances.

One pivotal event in particular that would determine the course of his future was the sudden death of his father when he was just eight years old. His dad, Sydney Wilson, went to work one day and never came home. My dad was forbidden to attend his funeral, and my grandma never spoke of it again. She never remarried and never took her wedding ring off until the day she died, over forty-five years later. It wasn't unusual back in those days that families would not speak of traumatic events – it all got swept under the carpet and all too often was left unprocessed. The attitude towards trauma was to keep it hidden – to bury it away as deep as possible so the ugly and painful feelings might not ever see the light of day. This deeply traumatic event at such a young age has stayed with my dad until this day, and although it has affected him in many negative ways, I am absolutely certain it was this pain that enabled him to manifest an unwavering determination and focus to succeed at life. It's truly inspiring to witness.

Following the death of my grandad, long before my own birth, my grandma was left raising her four children alone. A strong, hardworking, stoic woman, she played the part of the strict grandma – the one we were all a little bit scared of. She was tiny, but she was feisty. As a child, I never looked forward to going to her house the same way I did my other grandma's. We just couldn't relax in the same way. I always remember feeling 'on guard' and this sense that it was impossible to get close to her, as if there was this invisible shield around her that couldn't be penetrated. Through my young, innocent eyes, all I saw was an angry and unhappy woman who made everything we did as children seem regimented and difficult. Now, through my much wiser eyes, I can see that she had suffered in the most unimaginable ways; she was probably plagued with anxiety and undiagnosed depression, and carrying around deep repressed trauma. She had quite literally closed her heart off to the world. What I didn't know for many years was that even at the moment of her birth, tragedy struck, when her own mother died during childbirth. Years later, she went on to lose two children of her own – one at nine months old – and this was all before the loss of her beloved husband. The grief she felt must have been unbearable. As Oprah Winfrey says, in her book of the same name, we shouldn't be asking 'What's wrong with you?' – we should be asking 'What happened to you?'.

Despite the hardships of my dad's childhood, he never stopped believing in himself and his abilities. His strong work ethic, passed down by his mother and father, and his steely determination and desire to strive in life meant that not long after joining a local foundry in his first apprentice job, he would quickly take the plunge and start his own business. He built it from scratch, taking incredible risks and at times feeling like he was flying by the seat of his pants – but he had the solid belief that he could make it work. My mum, a qualified secretary, worked alongside my dad while raising four children and volunteering at the local youth club. They had a remarkably busy life, but it was a life they had chosen on their own terms, and they were determined to make the most of it. It was instilled in us early on that there was always something more to strive for in life; not necessarily material things, but personal growth. How far can you push yourself, challenge yourself? What can you learn from the challenges life throws at you? They didn't just preach it; they practised it right in front of us when faced with serious health challenges and the like. It's what I admire about them the most.

In August 1988, following a couple of burglaries at our home which left my mum feeling understandably vulnerable, my parents made the decision to move away for a new life in the countryside, so we packed up and moved to a tiny village in the Yorkshire Dales, a place called Airton. A pretty ballsy move for my Mum and Dad to make at the time. They had never left the place they grew up in, and it felt like a long way from everything they had known. But my dad, with his ability to master any challenge thrown at him, was ready to tackle this new start with both hands. I recall the day my parents took the four of us to view the new house. It was a small and what can only be described as derelict bungalow, and as I stepped inside, I remember thinking my parents had completely lost their minds. As we walked through the front door, we turned left through an archway into the main living area, where we were greeted by an old man with snowy white hair and beard, sitting in a rocking chair next to a small crackling open fire. The floorboards were completely bare, and the walls were crumbling. There was a faint smell of damp and mould, but strangely I felt a great sense of comfort there. The old man stood up from his chair and muttered a muffled hello under his breath; he was incredibly quiet and spoke with an age-induced stammer. Of course, nine-year-old me found this scary– he appeared to me like the one of those trolls found under bridges that you read about in children's books. I was cautious and followed my mum's lead. Clutching hands tightly, we wandered around each room, and I can remember wondering how on earth we all would fit in this tiny house– but I trusted my parents implicitly.

And I was right to trust them, as this turned out to be one of my favourite places in the whole world. I am still to this day so grateful to have grown up in the fresh country air, with most of our weekends taken up with walks by the river and riding our bikes. It was free from the city traffic, and we were constantly surrounded by endless rolling fields. This was before mobile phones and social media, of course; the internet had only just started to seep into our lives, and not everyone had it. So we were completely disconnected from technology and entirely connected to nature. We never knew just how good we had it. We had real conversations and felt a real sense of belonging. It was a simple life, and that life was good.

POLLYANNA VERSUS MRS THATCHER

I was lucky enough to grow up with parents who loved each other deeply. Mum and Dad met in 1970 and married soon after, in 1972. Mum was eighteen and Dad twenty-one and, as with most families back then, they had their two-point-four children in the first couple of years of marriage. My elder brothers, Ben and Dylan, were born in quick succession, just twenty-one months apart. My mum would often dress them in the same outfits, and they were (and still are) known as 'the boys' – I always think of them as Mum and Dad's first family. It was the perfect little family they had always hoped for, and life was good. Dad was continuing to build a successful business and had no desire to hear the pitter-patter of tiny feet again – but Mum was desperate to add more to her brood. Having children was her calling – her purpose in life, as she saw it. She couldn't escape or ignore the deep inner need to nurture and share her maternal love, and she wasn't afraid to fight for it. She would spend the next three years battling to convince my dad to have more children.

Now, to know my mum is to know a walking piece of divine compassion, empathy, and unconditional love. She will more often than not avoid confrontation and concede in most arguments – in part due to her kind and caring nature, but also due to never being encouraged to speak up as a child. So it was clear by her protest that this was going to be a deal-breaker in her marriage. It was a deeply upsetting time for both of them.

Then, in 1979, she finally got her wish: her first and only girl was born. And just like the then newly elected (and first) female prime minister, Margaret Thatcher, I came into the world with a hell of a lot to say. My mum often recalls what the midwife said in response to my loud cries upon entering the world.

'Are you breastfeeding, Mrs Wilson?'

'Yes, of course!'

The midwife sharply replied, 'Well for goodness' sake hurry up and stick her on!'

As a child I was often compared with Mrs Thatcher. I wouldn't keep quiet, I was determined, stubborn and had extraordinarily strong opinions. My parents would joke that I had the ability to win any argument; they weren't wrong. It reminds me of Mrs Thatcher's famous words from her Conservative Party conference in 1980: in response to expectations of her changing her mind on economic policies, she said, 'To those waiting with bated breath for that favourite media catchphrase, the U-turn, I have only one thing to say. You turn if you want to. The lady's not for turning.'

I was never for turning. I was always seen as a challenge, and over time I began to adopt the belief that the labels I had been given must be true. Despite sensing that these traits were not particularly desirable, I still relished the opportunity to gain attention from the adults in my life by acting out the labels. You see, I genuinely believe that at the core of all human beings is a fundamental need to be loved. We are born bathed in pure natural love and compassion, and it's only the world around us and the environments we find ourselves in that can transform this love into fear. Essentially, we are taught fear, but love is our true nature. I was desperately searching for that love in others in the only way I knew how, and that was to seek approval and validation. I would do whatever it took to be a 'good girl', and that meant meeting the expectations of others rather than myself. In truth, at my core and in my heart, I was quite the opposite to Mrs Thatcher. I was more like Pollyanna: soft, sensitive, kind-hearted, and forever the optimist. I always saw the best in everyone and from an early age I sought peace in every situation – until the world taught me I couldn't.

Even as a young adult I was told that my dreams of a peaceful world were a wonderful idealism, but not realistic

– leaving me feeling deflated. One song embodies just how I felt then and still feel about life now – 'Imagine' by John Lennon. His genius lyrics convey such a simple approach to life. And as I listened to those lyrics as a youngster, I knew I was a dreamer, and John reminded me that I wasn't the only one. It hollered the truth to me – something I felt completely aligned with. Looking back, that song was the foundation for the hope and faith which I would carry throughout my life.

Nevertheless, the world had already made up its mind who I should be, what I should believe in, and how I should or should not show my emotions. As a form of survival, I gradually learnt to adopt the 'Iron Lady' persona. This wasn't something that consciously happened; it was organic and instinctive. I became the classic people-pleaser. And with that, I had to cover up my true self and live a lie as my false self. In later years, my mum would call it my 'iron mask.' I often wonder now whether those loud screams and cries at birth were in fact my response to the world around me. You see, I've come to realise over recent years that I am a highly sensitive person (an HSP). This trait, as described by Elaine Aron in her book *The Highly Sensitive Person*, means I become overstimulated and sense the world around me at a much deeper level than most, which for HSPs means they are empaths in the truest sense of the word. I feel everything. Not just my own feelings, but the feelings of others. Not just the general compassion we all feel when we see someone suffering; for me it's a physical reaction to the energies of others around me which can be overwhelming, particularly as a child. It has taken me until my forties to be able to name these feelings and understand them at a deeper level.

As a child I was often told I was dramatic, sensitive, irrational, and moody. This made my school years difficult. I was often misunderstood. I felt as if I had been born with nerves on the outside of my body. Everyday life was an emotional overload, and from a young age I seemed to live in a state of confusion about my feelings and I didn't know what to do with them. They were big feelings for a small person. I tried to push them away, bury them, do anything I could to avoid them, afraid that those feelings would bubble up and make a mess for everyone.

I recall when I was around the age of six or seven my mum began taking me to the doctor on a regular basis as I was complaining of continuous stomach aches. The diagnosis was always the same: stomach migraines. In other words, the doctors didn't have a clue. I had repeated night terrors, waking in the middle of the night screaming, with no memory during or after the event; a common symptom of the HSP. Around the age of twelve, one Sunday afternoon on a trip back from my grandma's house, I fell asleep sitting in the back seat of my dad's red Renault Alpine – not unusual – but then out of nowhere I woke up and was instantly, visibly distressed for no apparent reason. Nothing had happened, but I was in floods of tears and shaking. My little brother, Syd, was sitting next to me, and despite him trying to comfort me and repeatedly asking me what was wrong, I just couldn't explain what was happening to me. These kinds of episodes went on for years. They still happen now occasionally, but now

I understand them and therefore the power behind them is dispelled much faster.

My need to 'hold myself together' would show up in strange ways, like the way I used to wrap my belt around my waist so tightly that Mum thought I would cut off my blood supply. It was a way of staying in control and preventing the dissociation from my body – I wasn't consciously aware of it at the time, of course, but I can see now how I was trying to manage my emotions by physically ensuring things around me felt tightly controlled. My parents did everything they could to love and support me and make me feel safe, but the reality is that for the most part we have all been raised with the 'reward or punishment' model of parenting. They were no different to their own parents, and likely their parents before them. Don Miguel Ruiz refers to this as 'domesticating' children. He writes in his book *The Four Agreements*:

> *Children are domesticated the same way that we domesticate a dog, a cat, or any other animal. In order to teach a dog, we punish the dog, and we give it rewards. We train our children whom we love so much the same way that we train any domesticated animal: with a system of punishment and reward . . . The reward is the attention we got from our parents or from other people like siblings, teachers, and friends . . . We try to please Mum and Dad, we try to please the teachers at school, we try to please the church, and so we start acting.*

I was an excellent actor. And it turned out my little brother was, too.

Four years after my birth, at the beginning of 1983, my parents had what they refer to as a 'slip-up' and discovered they were expecting another child. Unlike with the pregnancy that resulted in me, my dad seemed overjoyed to be becoming a father again. So much so that he began choosing baby names immediately. They tried to keep the pregnancy their little secret for a while, until one day a plumber came to the house to fix the central heating. After my mum showed him to the kitchen and offered him a cup of tea, he said in his broad Yorkshire accent, 'Is thee in t' family way again, Mrs Wilson?'

Fat chance they could keep it a secret when even the local plumber could spot her bulging tummy. So, it was announced to close family and friends that there was to be a fourth addition to the Wilson family. Little did they know just what an impact this one was going to make on all of us.

Mum had a difficult pregnancy and felt discomfort from the very moment she found out she was expecting my brother. This was in the days before ultrasound scans; she instead had a midwife visit her at home to do physical examinations. When they came to measure her about halfway through the pregnancy, she was told it was likely she would be having twins. Although my mum can't recall now exactly what was said, she remembers that she and my dad were so convinced they would be welcoming two bundles of joy that they bought extra nappies and babygrows.

Four weeks before her due date, her waters broke unexpectedly. Back then it was quite frightening to be delivering so early, so once my grandparents had arrived to look after the three of us, my dad rushed her to the hospital, where she endured an awfully long and traumatic labour. When my brother finally arrived, it was clear he had been in serious trouble; my mum recalls how blue he was. After a brief touch, he was whisked away into the neonatal intensive care unit, where he would stay for two days, my mum only being allowed in once to give him his first bath. This was, understandably, extremely distressing for her. He weighed 7lb 4oz, an unusually heavy baby at thirty-six weeks. It was also clear from the size of the umbilical cord and placenta that the midwife had been right all along, and he had started out as a twin.

A few days later, Louis Sydney Wilson – aka Syd – my baby brother, finally came home. I remember feeling like all my Christmases had come at once. My own real-life doll. My excitement was overflowing, and I just couldn't wait to hold him. I was just four years old, and I was the happiest little girl in the world. Joyously helping my mum with nappy changing and dressing him, I was in my element. I loved him so much it made me want to cry. He was wearing his brand-new white outfit – lovingly knitted by my Gran, complete with matching bootees – and I posed for the camera, cradling him in my arms. Oozing pride out of every pore, I remember thinking it was the best day of my life.

Syd was a super cute kid. He had the cheekiest smile and

was always happy. My brothers and I would often dress him up in hats and coats that didn't fit him, and because of his calm and quiet demeanour he didn't seem fazed at all; he just stood there staring with his big blue eyes, wondering what all the laughter and fuss was about. I took my role of big sister very seriously, and always felt that I was his second mother. I was my mum's faithful little helper. Wherever Syd was, I would go too. In photos I am often seen standing next to or behind him, always the protector.

Whenever we took the long drive (it was only an hour but felt like five) back from our grandparents' house on the weekend, I can remember Mum giving me clear instructions to not let Syd go to sleep. She would repeat over and over 'No go leepies, no go leepies,' then she would get all of us to join in. I would tap his face gently or stroke his hand lovingly, trying to keep him awake as best I could. When he would start to drift off into a deep slumber, we would all start chanting again in unison, 'No go leepies, Louis, no go leepies.' This performance often continued the whole way home. It wasn't until I became a parent that I finally had an appreciation as to why my mum was so desperate to keep him awake.

With such a big age gap between him and the rest of us, we would tease him like all good siblings, telling him he was an accident and adopted, or he was the milkman's son. Classic sibling rivalry. We teased him for being the favourite, the 'golden child'. The truth was, we were all jealous. He was born at a time when my parents were more comfortable financially than when we were born, so it always appeared that he had more than we did – but of course this didn't mean he was loved any more or less than us. This sort of behaviour wasn't unusual for a family of four children all battling for attention, love, and their place in the family hierarchy.

In contrast, I was the only girl, in a house – and a world – dominated by boys. It felt hard to breathe sometimes. My highly sensitive trait made it difficult for me to express my emotions. I was teased and taunted, poked and prodded, and my naivete meant I fell for lots of practical jokes at home and at school. These experiences were genuinely painful for me. I was vulnerable and became an easy target for the bullies. I would try desperately to hide how hurt I was, and only ever broke down once in front of my mum when the teasing became too much to bear.

I can recall that day very clearly. I returned home from school, and as I disembarked from the school bus and greeted my mum, she could see the depth of sadness in my eyes. On the journey home that afternoon, I had been excluded from sitting with anyone on the school bus, so took a seat on my own. As I stared out of the window, I overheard two of the girls discussing their 'I Hate Kay Wilson' folder. Yes, you heard that right – an actual folder where they would keep notes on how much they hated me and why. I could hear them giggling and sniggering as they added more hurtful comments about the way I wore my clothes, the type of bag I brought to school, the way I walked . . . the list went on. How could anyone hate another person so much for no real reason? Maybe there was something wrong with me. As I sat there on my own with my head hanging down, wishing the world would swallow me whole, I felt an enormous ball of shame hit the pit of my stomach. I would do anything to make that feeling go away. I needed acceptance. I needed to belong.

Even after those difficult years at middle school, my Pollyanna attitude meant I was forever hopeful that something would change, that things would get better. I picked myself up and focused on the next chapter. High school was just around the corner, and there would be a whole new group of people there from other schools in the local community. But what I didn't know then was that something else was on the horizon that would define my teenage years.

CHRISTMAS

At the age of thirty-six, following complications from the difficulties of carrying her four babies, my mum experienced a prolapse of her womb and required an immediate hysterectomy, with both her womb and ovaries being removed. This launched her into early menopause – daunting and traumatic for a young, otherwise fit and healthy woman – and to make matters worse, over several months she unknowingly received an accidental overdose of oestrogen from the doctors who were supposed to be taking care of her. Following this, her body went into toxic shock – and in 1993, just before Christmas, she almost died.

I can still remember visiting her at the hospital. I was anxious and frightened about what was happening. Even though I was assured by my dad that all would be OK, I couldn't stop the fear creeping in. As I entered the room and cautiously approached the bed, I was horrified to find a pile of skin that had been shed from her feet like potato peelings. Not only that – it was purple. I vaguely remember someone trying to explain that this was dye from the disinfectant baths they were using. Nevertheless, it didn't calm my insides one iota. My mum looked empty as she lay exhausted in bed. She looked beaten both physically and emotionally, and I couldn't imagine how she would make it home for Christmas. How would we cope? In my mind, Mum was the centre of our world. I couldn't see how life would function at home without her. How would Dad function without her?

To put things into context, my relationship with my dad when I was a child was the polar opposite from where it is now. I always knew he loved me, but often his actions and words (or lack of words, at times) made me feel unloved, ignored, and even abandoned. I believe these feelings towards my dad began as early as the womb. By my mum's own admission, he ignored her during her pregnancy with me. He was still nursing his wounds from the battle he had lost, and couldn't face the impending arrival of the third child he didn't want. The upset and stress my mum must have endured during this time had left an imprint on the growing foetus inside her. And even when I finally arrived, my dad still didn't seem interested. Physical touch from him was non-existent for the majority of the first two years of my life.

Now, you're probably thinking 'What kind of man could do that? Ignore his wife, ignore his own child?' but I have learnt over time that this was never about me. It wasn't personal. It was merely a projection of my dad's own fears and insecurities, stemming from his own childhood. He had lost control, and he didn't like it. He was the strict disciplinarian, and I was raised like many children in the eighties, whereby if you were in trouble, you would dread those famous words coming from your mother's mouth: 'Just you wait until your dad gets home'. His love for me was expressed in many ways – but it wasn't in the way that leaves you feeling soft and fuzzy. He showed his love by working hard to provide a beautiful life for us. He taught me how to show up in the world – with all you've got! He taught me how to ride a bike, drive a car, run a business, and to always do the right thing, no matter the cost. His sheer determination and focus to keep us all together was undeniable. But Mum was my anchor of love. There was no getting away from it. And the thought of her being out of the picture frightened me immensely. She had been my constant, our bond so strong from the womb; she was the one I went to for emotional stability. She gave me unconditional love and affection. She was soft, warm, and nurturing, and she made me feel safe. But in 1993 it was like I had the rug pulled from underneath me. I lost my safe place.

After much persuasion, the hospital finally agreed to let my mum go home on Christmas Eve. She was a broken woman, but she refused to be away from her beloved family at Christmastime. Christmas has always been a special time for us. Just as for a lot of families, it conjures up feelings of to-getherness, love, and happiness. Nothing else seems to mat-ter, and all rules go out of the window. A glass of champagne at 9 a.m.? Sure, why not! Chocolate treats at 8 a.m., kids? Absolutely! I was so excited about my mum's return home on Christmas Eve. I was desperate for some normality, and having her home would surely mean happy times once again. But it just wasn't to be. One aspect of her illness I did not and could not have understood at the tender age of thirteen was the highs and very deep lows of the hormonal imbalances she was experiencing and their effect on her brain. In the year be-fore and the year after, I would briefly mention her struggles in my diary – like in July 1992, when I wrote: 'My Mum was crying when I got home, but I don't know what for?' And two years later in July 1994: 'Mum spent most of the day in her room bawling her eyes out.'

I know Mum and Dad did everything they could to pro-tect all four of us from what was happening, and they would try to explain what they thought was appropriate – always trying to balance the truth with protection– but the reality for me at the time was a feeling of confusion, abandonment, and fear. We would argue about the smallest, most insignifi-cant things; it would blow up from nowhere.

Joe Dispenza, author of *Breaking the Habit of Being Yourself*, says that 'memories are imprinted in our cells be-cause they are related to a heightened emotional experience'. I believe this wholeheartedly. Christmas Eve in 1993 was one of those memories for me.

I watched as Mum settled herself on the couch next to the fireplace and Dad poured her a large glass of whisky and placed it on the coffee table beside her. The doorbell rang; it was the local butcher, delivering the fresh produce for Christmas Day and the week ahead. Normally an exciting time in our house. My mum got up from her chair, noticeably wobbly, and greeted the lady at the door. I was standing next to her, partly as protection and partly curious as to what delicious treats the woman may be bearing. As my mum checked through the items, she noticed something was wrong with the delivery. I forget now exactly what was missing from the order – perhaps the fish, but it doesn't matter; the point to note here is that under normal circumstances this would be a minor inconvenience and would be settled with an apology. But for my mum and her poor out-of-balance body and mind, it was too much to deal with. It was the straw that broke the camel's back that Christmas Eve. I watched in shock and disbelief as she unleashed her venom on the innocent woman. I don't recall exactly what my mum said, but it included a lot of profanities she never used in her everyday life. She shouted and screamed so loudly at this woman it scared me. I didn't recognise her. Feelings of shame and embarrassment arose inside me, and I scurried off as quickly as I could to my room. I sat crouched next to my dressing table with my hands covering my ears, desperate for someone to make it all go away.

The next morning, Christmas Day, I visited my mum's bedroom reluctantly, unsure what mood would greet me. All

I wanted was for her to get up and for everything to go back to how it was. I could feel myself drifting further and further away from her – she was no longer my anchor, and I was feeling adrift at sea with no shore in sight.

OFF THE RAILS

By the time I started high school, I had become accustomed to wearing my 'iron mask' for protection, and I had realised that, as the old saying goes: 'if you can't beat them, join them'. And so began the long and unconscious process of losing myself. I began smoking and drinking at thirteen years old. Not the best move for an HSP, but I've since discovered it's a survival plan adopted by many.

In the UK it isn't unusual for most young people to dabble with drinking and smoking, but as I have reflected over time, I've come to realise that we are conditioned by the culture we are born into; in our case, that it is perfectly acceptable, and even encouraged, to drink copious amounts of alcohol in particular. My parents drank and their parents drank; everybody, it seemed, drank. My mum smoked, too, so surely that was fine? Drinking at such an early age as a form of both escape and acceptance was dangerous, but I see now it was my coping mechanism. I can see how desperate I was to seek validation from outside of myself. I started looking for love in all the wrong places. I was taken advantage of many times. I knew I had so much more to give, but nobody wanted to talk about the same things that I did, so I took the path of least resistance. It was easier to join in the gossip and escape my true self by using alcohol, cigarettes – and later, for a brief period, recreational drugs. The trouble with all this pretending was that it meant I was often misunderstood by others. I was smart, kind, and thoughtful on the inside, yet on the outside I would often come across as stuck-up, cold, arrogant, self-righteous, opinionated, and stubborn. My protective shield, although comfortable for me, would often push others away, leaving me even more alone than before.

By 1996, at the age of seventeen, I had left school without any sort of plan for my future. I had been sacked from my first job, with an insurance company. I was in an abusive relationship and had left home, devastating my parents. I was behaving totally out of character, and I could feel myself falling down a slippery – albeit well-hidden – slope. I was far too proud and ashamed to admit that I was struggling. I was hiding a life of physical and emotional abuse and I was finding myself in situations that were dangerous and risky. I was a culturally trained people-pleaser, so of course I would do anything for those I loved, even if it meant putting myself in danger. On one occasion, I found myself an accidental accomplice to an armed robbery. My sheer naivete meant I fell for the story that my boyfriend and I were going out for a drive to pick up takeaway food and then back to his house. As we were pulled over by the police that cold, wet Sunday evening, I had no idea what was happening. My boyfriend told me, of course, that nothing was wrong and that I should just stay quiet – but of course the lies eventually came pouring out when he was subsequently arrested: the date and time matched with the trip to the takeaway. What a fool I was. I still didn't leave, though. I continued to forgive him repeatedly for what felt like hundreds of faux pas. He crossed the line, and eventually I would step over it with him like a 'good girl'. The pattern continued. I genuinely believed that things would change – he would change. If only I knew then what I know now. Hindsight is a wonderful thing!

One day in mid 1996 the first stitch in my well put-together life finally came undone. I awoke around 8 a.m. at the house I was sharing with my boyfriend and a couple of his friends. For the very first time in my life, I had a sense that I could hear my own true inner voice. It was noticeably separate from my normal thoughts. It was distinct, clear, and purposeful. It reminds me now of some words that my mum had written in a diary she gave me almost ten years later. It said: 'When you are weak, down, and out, think of God and give him a shout. He's the only person that is never out.'

That inner voice I could hear that day was my interpretation of God. And it said very clearly, 'Kay, it's time to go home' – and just like that, I went home.

I waited for my boyfriend to go to work, packed all of my belongings, and called my dad to come and collect me. I can remember walking into the house rather sheepishly and stepping into my bedroom again for the first time – the familiar smells of Mum's cooking, everything so warm and cosy and, most importantly, safe. It was my safe place.

I decided to sort my life out and return to the local college to study business for two years. I had this inner knowing that I had so much more to do with my life and that the road I had been on was leading to a dead end or, even worse, a cataclysmic disaster. It makes me shudder even now to think where I could be now had I not listened to my inner voice that day.

Things didn't get better straight away. I continued my relationship with my boyfriend for another eighteen months; I was too afraid to leave and just couldn't seem to find a way out. Anyone who has experienced this type of relationship will understand that leaving is the hardest thing to do. So I continued to lie to myself and my family.

Then in August of 1998, my world came crashing down: my grandad was diagnosed with bowel cancer and died within six weeks of diagnosis, my grandma fell and broke her hip and died two weeks later, and a good friend from school was killed in a car accident at the tender age of nineteen. This all happened in the space of three weeks. It felt too much to bear. My sensitive soul couldn't deal with the enormity of the loss I was experiencing, and I fell into what I now recognise as my first acute depressive episode.

By nature, I am a deep thinker – melancholic, even, at times – but this was the first time I had experienced not being able to function well enough to get out of bed in the morning. I couldn't speak without bursting into tears. I had no idea what was happening to me and so I turned to my mum for help. She knocked on the door one morning and I reluctantly let her in. As she entered my bedroom, she gave me a sympathetic look and offered to contact the place where I worked to explain the situation – I had only been at my new job a few months and was still on probation. I was so worried I would lose my job. She then bundled me into the car and took me to see a homeopath. I didn't know much about homeopathy at the time; I just knew Mum had started seeing one after her near-death episode and it seemed to help, so I was open to trying anything. We made the fifteen-minute drive over the windy roads to Settle, the same town where we all went to school. As we pulled up next to the drystone wall across from his house, I can remember feeling a sense of anxiety, but knowing my mum was there made me feel safe and secure. I took a deep breath and walked in.

I don't remember the entire conversation we had – only that I still struggled to speak without crying – but his sense of compassion and care was like nothing I had experienced before. It never felt like that at the GP surgery. He was so thorough, and it felt more like a counselling session. I left after about an hour with a small bag of little pills to take – I really didn't hold out much hope of them working, but I trusted my mum and I was desperate to feel normal again.

Within seven days I was like a different person. I was back at work and feeling like I could take on the world once again. The grief I was experiencing was still there, but it was manageable, and I could function in everyday life again. But as I slipped back into being a fully functioning human, I could sense something inside of me had shifted. Something fundamental. Something clicked, and I started to question everything. It was like I had opened my eyes for the first time, like someone had grabbed me by the shoulders and shaken me, shouting 'wake up, wake up!' until I paid attention. Life was calling me to change my path. I had to get out of the abusive relationship, regardless of the consequences. I had to have faith that it would all work out. And just like my inner voice two years earlier, I listened once again, and left that relationship, and broke free. Looking back now, I can see how this was a defining moment. There were consequences I had to face, but they would lead to the next important chapter of my life.

PARALLELS

Unlike me, Syd had a wonderful time at school, and he continued to go with the flow. He had an amazing group of friends; everyone loved him. He was such a happy-go-lucky kind of kid. He never took anything too seriously and was completely unaware of my difficulties at the time. My acting skills really paid off.

When Syd was born, in 1983, the world was taking giant leaps in the progress of digital technology. We were all in awe when the first CD players hit the shops. It seemed incomprehensible that we could really play music this way; no need to fast forward or rewind our favourite albums any more– just skip. It was like magic! No more cassette tapes with reams of tape pulled out and ruined in the tape player when it got stuck trying to record the Top Forty on a Sunday evening.

Straight from the womb, Syd had always shown a keen interest and curiosity in how things worked, and as he grew older he wanted to understand technology and the engineering of everything from a cruise ship to a racing car. He was forever inquisitive. In particular, he would marvel at the abilities of any human being who demonstrated sheer talent and genius-like qualities.

On 16th May 1983, the entire world was captivated by Michael Jackson's famous moonwalk. I'm not one hundred per cent sure whether my parents sat me in front of the TV that night, but every time I watch that clip, I can sense the reaction that would have rippled among the other forty-seven million people watching. He appeared superhuman as he glided across that stage. His music became an integral part of our young lives, and Syd most definitely idolised him. Those were the sorts of people that inspired him – the greats, the masters of their skill. His ultimate hero, though, was the racing driver Ayrton Senna. As with most people who idolise someone, Syd recognised aspects of himself in Ayrton: he was a deep thinker, a private man, determined, disciplined, and focused. His sharp mind and kind and generous heart struck a chord with Syd, who would later name his son after him.

When Syd was just thirteen, he took up go-karting as a hobby, inspired by Dad's early career as a rally driver – and, just like Dad, he took to it like a duck to water. The passion for driving is in our blood, and for Syd, when he hit the track it became a spiritual experience. He would describe it as connecting to his true self. He was transported to another world – a world that made sense and where every part of his being felt truly aligned. He was 'in the zone'.

After showing real talent, he began racing competitively at sixteen years old. He was a natural, quick and fearless behind the wheel. He always seemed older than his years, and by the time he was seventeen he was racing at various meetings all around the country. He raced with, and often won against, many talented drivers, including a young Lewis Hamilton. It was an exciting time. At eighteen years of age, he entered the Renault Clio sporting club and received local sponsorship. He did well in coming up through the ranks – but then, at the famous Rockingham racetrack in Northampton, his racing days ended. He finished in the top ten. His talent was clear to anyone watching. Eventually, following their deliberation, the judges whittled it down from the top ten to the top five. He heard his name announced – he made it! The next step was for the overall winner to be selected from the top five. He waited patiently, anticipating his name being called again; he had no reason not to be confident, because he'd had the drive of his life . . . but his dreams were shattered when another racing driver was selected as the winner.

It's no secret that in order to progress in motor racing, a substantial amount of financial investment is required. The harsh reality was that my parents couldn't afford what was required to get Syd where he needed to be. Not only that, but over time Syd had slowly become disillusioned with the sport. It was a sport in which it appeared 'money talks' – and it seemed to speak a lot louder than talent. This didn't sit well with him – it messed with his moral compass, and he just couldn't bring himself to continue competing when he thought the decisions being made were unfair and unjust. His career in racing ended that day at Rockingham. He was devastated. Motor sport was something he always wanted to return to in the future in some capacity, but at that time it wasn't meant to be. His passion for cars, however, never went away. What he didn't know about cars wasn't worth knowing. He had a brain like a computer, filing away every piece of engineering knowledge about almost any car you could think of, ready to recall at any moment. He and my dad shared this obsession, and I would love to watch them both enthralled in conversation about their favourite topic.

Syd, in his own words, had a dream childhood. He loved everything about his life in those tender years. Things, however, started to change for him after he stopped racing. He had lost his mojo and wasn't sure where his life was heading. He was confused, and his disillusionment continued. At the age of twenty-one he started to slip down the same slippery hole I had fallen into and became sucked into the dreaded fate of living his life to please others. His story and mine ran parallel to each other, but we wouldn't discover the patterns and synchronicities until many years later.

CHAPTER THREE: HIGH SKIES AND BLACK HOLES

A ship is always safe at the shore,
but that is not what it is built for.
Albert Einstein

In February 1999 I met and fell instantly in love with the man who would later become my husband: Richard Paul Backhouse (Rick). I was nineteen and he was turning twenty-six the following month. Something magical happened that chilly night in February. A random get-together with a friend I hadn't seen in months led me straight into the path of this handsome, cheeky, loveable rogue who would change my life forever. We talk about that night often. We both felt a surging magnetic force pulling us together. As clichéd as it may sound, it felt like electricity between us. I was in no doubt that he was 'the one' – and in May 1999, just three months after our first meeting, he asked me to become his wife. Everyone thought we were crazy. We were, but we didn't care; it felt so right. It was an exciting time – we were young and very much in love – but there were early challenges ahead.

On 20th March 2000, Rick's dad – my father-in-law, John Henry Backhouse – died tragically following a battle with depression and alcoholism. I was six months pregnant with our first son, Louis. Rick and I had only been together just over a year. It was a traumatic time. I can still remember that Sunday evening as clear as day. His dad had been to visit us the night before, which was extremely unusual. It had been Rick's birthday a few weeks prior, and we had just moved into our first home together. This was to be his first and only visit. He turned up unexpectedly as we were tucking into our habitual weekly Chinese takeaway. He wasn't keen to eat with us and instead opted for a cup of tea. I remember sitting on the wall in our back garden as he smoked a cigarette and sipped his tea. He wasn't a big talker. I had only known him a year, but I had already worked out that he was a reserved and private man. I can't remember exactly what we talked about that evening; however, I do remember the ease in our conversation and his quiet sense of pride as he sat in our new home, glancing at my pregnant belly. He even brought a handwritten card with him, which read: 'Happy Birthday Rik, Love Dad xx p.s. good luck to you both in your new home.'

There's something so special about another person's handwriting. It's as if you can sense the spirit of that person being transmitted through the words on the paper.

I felt so grateful that he came to visit that evening, and that by some miracle he'd even attended our wedding just three months earlier. At the time, he had been in and out of hospital following a suicide attempt, and was being treated for depression in the psychiatric unit. We honestly didn't think he would make it to the wedding. We had visited several times, and each time it was the same little awkward dance.

He sat for a while, we spoke briefly, but the conversation was always uncomfortable, neither party knowing what to say. He would go outside to smoke, and then we left. My skills in managing another person's depression were well below par at that time. I just remember feeling very sad and helpless about the whole situation. I trusted that he was in the right place and would get the help he needed and eventually get better. So it truly meant the world to us when he requested to be discharged for the day so that he could be by our side on our special day. I often look at his beaming smile in our wedding photographs and think how important that day was for him – and for us. He didn't have to say anything; his face said it all. We had no idea that just three months later he would no longer be with us.

On the evening of 20th March 2000, at around 7.30 p.m., sitting on the end of the sofa, Rick turned to me and said, 'I think I'm going to give Dad a call.'

My instincts told me something was wrong. He was often worried about his dad, understandably, but on this particular evening I could see his anxiety was heightened. There was no answer. Before he left the house to check on him, I said, 'Ring Mick, darling. Don't go on your own.' Mick is his younger brother. He lived close by, and I didn't want Rick to be alone.

As he left the house, I sat there waiting, trying not to run all the scenarios through my head. Trying to distract myself with the television, making cups of tea, going to the bathroom – anything. Within twenty minutes or so, the front door burst open. It was Rick's auntie, who lived at the bottom of our street. She shouted hurriedly, 'He's dead! John's dead!'

My blood ran cold. I didn't know what to do. It all seemed to happen so quickly, and I just froze. He had died alone in his flat, just two hundred yards away from us. It was hard to comprehend that we had just spent the evening with him the night before and now he was gone. How could this have happened?

His official cause of death was a stomach ulcer and gastrointestinal haemorrhage, which the doctor told us was brought on by his alcoholism. My heart sank. Rick was devastated. John was just fifty-two years old.

I have no memory of the days between his death and the funeral. At just twenty years of age, I was carrying our first child and what felt like the weight of everyone's sadness. As I clutched my swollen belly, standing in the church pew, watching the coffin go by, I couldn't help but think this was a defining moment and would change the course of our lives together. This was supposed to be the happiest time of our lives. This wasn't how it was supposed to be. Depression had touched my life again – but this time it wasn't my own.

No one really knows how long John's depression plagued his life. The trouble with depression is that it's a silent killer; although society is now talking more openly about mental health and trying to remove the stigma, the reality is that the majority of people still suffer in silence. Men in particular find it much harder to talk about their feelings, often being conditioned to believe that it's weak to cry and being told to 'man up' or 'grow some balls'. They were taught that they should carry the responsibility of the entire family on their shoulders. To make matters worse, in the UK we are taught that we must keep a stiff upper lip – we must be strong and carry on regardless. The upper echelons of the monarchy have reinforced this by demonstrating that we must put duty and service before our feelings and emotions – thankfully, this is now changing, but there is still so much work to be done. With all of this pressure to keep it all together, how can we ever feel safe enough to fall apart? As a result, we have an epidemic on our hands of gargantuan proportions as our suicide rates now soar year on year, both in this country and globally. We are witnessing countless unnecessary deaths, and the impact on the loved ones of those suffering is often overlooked. From my own personal experience, I know that in order to break down the barriers to healing, we must create a safe space for others to share their vulnerabilities, insecurities, and emotions without the fear of shame or judgement.

My natural reaction following my father-in-law's death was, of course, to stay strong and keep my 'stiff upper lip'. I made damn sure that this was what everyone saw on the outside. Meanwhile, on the inside, I was scared and confused, and felt ill-equipped to handle the situation I found myself in. Rick had plummeted into his own depression, and although I did the best I could to offer my support, I found it more and more difficult to live with the roller coaster of emotions that came from living with someone following a deeply traumatic event that had cut them off at the knees. I didn't have the knowledge I have now, and often I would indirectly exacerbate the situation without knowing any better, leading to more pain for both of us. I tried my best to navigate my way through these circumstances that were new to me, but a lot of the time I just brushed everything under the carpet and hoped for the best. I had to stay strong, not only for Rick but for the new life that was growing in my tummy— so, for the next twelve years at least, the 'iron mask' stayed firmly in place; I never asked for help, believing I could (and should) fix everything myself. My childhood conditioning and circumstances meant that I would always go it alone. I was proud of my strength and survival; I wore them like a badge of honour.

I often think about how we celebrate the strength and resilience of other people, those who hold it all together. 'Isn't she amazing?' 'Isn't she so strong?' We often hold those people in the highest esteem – failing to realise that their apparent resilience often leaves those people avoiding their own pain. They never feel they have permission to crumble and fall. In my case, asking for help meant exposing my vulnerabilities; it meant people would see I wasn't perfect, which would shatter the illusion. This would mean failure. It was my biggest fear.

THE INVISIBLE CAGE

Do you ever wonder what your purpose in life is? I do; it's something I've thought about most of my life. I certainly know for sure what it isn't. It isn't following the societal norms or keeping up with the Joneses, and it most definitely isn't chasing anything outside of ourselves. All of those paths will only keep us small, when our natural inclination is to expand and be big. Just like the universe, we are forever changing, growing, and expanding – unless, of course, we choose to stay small.

I believe that from a young age we begin building an invisible cage around ourselves, filling it with all the things we think we are supposed to have, the things we're told will make us successful and happy: money, marriage, a house, cars, two point four children, the nine-to-five job, the two-week holiday once a year, the material possessions we are told we must have. But the reality, of course, is that none of these things can truly make us happy. How often do we hear people say they wish they could win the lottery, as if this would somehow fix their life? It just isn't true. Those things we fill our cages with can appear to be things that will make us happy, and they are definitely options we have available to us, but they're not the only options we have in life. Being the creatures of habit that we are, the majority of us tend to align ourselves with the way of life that mirrors the culture and society that surrounds us. But we should tread this path with caution. As I once heard Wayne Dyer at a speaking event say, 'If you follow the herd, you will end up stepping in shit!'

Speaking from my own experience, I can see that in my early adulthood I never truly questioned any of my decisions. I just blindly did what I had been taught to do. When did I stop asking questions? When did I stop being curious? I've traced this back to childhood. Children ask questions incessantly, particularly around the age of four or five. 'Why, why, why? But *why*, Mummy?' They repeat their questions over and over. If you're a parent reading this, you will know exactly what I mean. It's exhausting. All you want to do is to scream 'Be quiet!'.

So why do the majority of children stop asking questions?

Like many people today, I grew up in a time when children were expected to be seen and not heard. We were instructed by most of the adults in our lives to stay quiet and do as we were told – by our teachers, our religious leaders, our parents, our grandparents. We were taught that our voice was not as important as theirs. So our default position was to keep our thoughts and ideas, both good and bad, to ourselves. The adults in our lives didn't do this on purpose, of course. They loved us and wanted the best for us, but indirectly and unconsciously they would often teach us to suppress our true selves. The result? An inability of a substantial portion of the population to think for themselves, leading them to build a life that will please other people rather than themselves. This is the invisible cage.

The problem with an invisible cage, of course, is that it's invisible! In my case, I had no idea it was holding me back and tricking me into thinking I lived in a world that was small and offered what seemed like limited possibilities. I became small in my thinking. I had pigeonholed myself and created a list of labels describing what I was or wasn't, making my possibilities in life even smaller. I had told myself a story about who I was – and I was starting to believe it. Luckily for me, Rick held the key that would unlock the door to my invisible cage and release me into a world I didn't know existed beyond those walls.

THE LAND OF OZ

Everyone knows the story of *The Wizard of Oz*: the story of young Dorothy and her little dog, Toto, and their journey along the yellow brick road to find the Wizard of Oz in the Emerald City, who would help her and her friends the Scarecrow, the Tin Man, and the Lion to find a brain, a heart, some courage, and eventually a ticket home to Kansas. The 1939 film adaptation has held a special place in our family, as it's Rick's favourite childhood film. He can repeat every word, every song, and his feelings and memories associated with the film run deep. It wasn't until recently, though, that I thought about the spiritual meaning behind the film and its connection to my own life. Dorothy represents all of us living in our own black-and-white Kansas, searching for something more. We know intuitively that there is something better waiting for us 'over the rainbow'. But we can't tread someone else's yellow brick road; we have to forge our own path – the road less travelled – to raise our level of consciousness. Dorothy's friends along the way represent the things we must gather along our journey of self-discovery: knowledge, empathy, and courage – or what I later call purpose, love, and faith. When we finally reach the Emerald City— our personal utopia— Toto (our intuition) reveals that the wizard is in fact a fraud, and we learn, as the famous quote goes, that 'You've always had the power, dear; you've just had to learn it for yourself'.

In 2006 I found myself at the crossroads of my very own yellow brick road. I had to decide whether I was ready to take the road less travelled. Rick's depression and anxiety symptoms had worsened. By 2004 he was suffering from severe panic attacks which on occasion resulted in ambulance trips and admissions to hospital. He had become heavily reliant on alcohol to sleep, and what I didn't realise then but know now was that I had fallen into a habit of drinking heavily to escape my own pain and as a desperate attempt to stay close and connected to him.

By 2006 the pressure on our marriage was beginning to show. During a holiday to Tenerife in January, arguments turned into conversations about leaving the UK and moving our entire lives to the other side of the world – to Australia. A fresh start, a better life. It hadn't come completely out of nowhere; Rick had always hinted before we were even married that he wanted to live in another country, but I'd just figured he was talking nonsense and he wouldn't bring it up again. Maybe he was right, though? Maybe this would fix everything? As I sat in front of the computer looking at photos of houses with swimming pools and marvelling at the endless beaches, I couldn't deny the beauty I saw. But my fear of change would continually take over. The fear would rise slowly when I imagined a life without everything I had to come to know. How could I leave my family? How could I do that to them? How could I take my boys away from their grandparents, aunties, uncles, and cousins? How could I leave my job, having done the same thing for ten years? I didn't know anything else. As I saw it, I had the perfect life. I had everything that represented a successful life, and I was happy. Or so I thought.

Questions and thoughts plagued my mind for weeks and months before eventually Rick got his wish. The visas were granted, and the dominoes started falling. I could see that this was what he wanted and needed, and he assured me that our Emerald City would be waiting for us at the other side of the rainbow. It felt like make or break. I had to trust him and, despite the fear, I sensed there was something bigger than me at play and I should take a leap of faith. I had no idea why; it was just a deep knowing that the move would change the course of my life and that's what we needed. I had to listen to my inner voice once again.

Despite this inner knowing, it wasn't going to be easy. I had to dig deep. The majority of our family couldn't understand what we were doing or why we would leave. Arguments flared up between some members of the family, resulting in hurt and resentment. The guilt I felt was eating up my insides, and everybody else's tears became my own. It was understandable that they would be so upset; they loved us all so much, and our boys were so young. Even now, they will describe their feelings of grief after we left. What they didn't know was that I felt exactly the same way – but I had to keep the iron mask firmly in place. We were in too deep now, and staying was no longer an option. One conversation I can remember vividly was with Syd at our family farewell. We had been out for dinner at the Coniston Hotel – the same hotel where Rick and I were married. When we arrived back at my parents' home, and after taking snapshots of the family together one last time, Syd came and sat next to me on the sofa and said something along the lines of, 'I can't believe you're leaving all of your family and everything you know – why would you do that? Don't you think you're a little crazy?'

Then he reminded me of some lyrics from the song 'Everybody's Free' by Baz Luhrmann, the words about getting to know your parents, because you never know when they'll be gone for good. And how you should stick with your siblings because they're most likely to be around in the future.

I could feel a mixture of anger and guilt swirling around in my stomach. How could he make me feel so guilty? He had no idea what I was going through or how much I wanted to scream for the entire process to stop – but how could he have known? I never told him.

When we talked about this conversation years later, he explained how desperate he had been for me to stay due to his own unhappiness with life at the time. I had no idea. By lying to ourselves and each other, we had created huge misunderstandings. He had been wearing a mask too – just like me.

Leaving the UK was preceded by some of the most difficult moments of my life. Saying goodbye to my family and friends felt like attending a funeral every day for two weeks straight. I was distraught, and it was exhausting. The weight of the iron mask was taking its toll. Rick was in a vastly different place to me and seemed oblivious to the pain I was experiencing; he'd mapped out his escape route, and nothing was going to change his mind. We often recall the moment we left my mother-in-law's house on the morning of our departure. As I sat there staring bleary-eyed at the four suitcases and our two young children, thinking *What the hell are we doing?*, he was busy marvelling at the interior of the Mercedes-Benz minivan that picked us up. 'It's so cool, isn't it?' he said, excitedly.

I couldn't respond. Were we even on the same planet?

As we arrived at Manchester Airport, I made a beeline for the nearest bar. I knocked back a large glass of wine with a Valium on the side as swiftly as I could – my fear of flying still overwhelmed every part of my being, so today was anxiety on steroids. The boys were completely unaware of their mother falling apart at the seams and smiled from ear to ear for their final photo on British soil; my hands shook as I held the camera. It started to feel like this was all happening to someone else, as if I were floating around, watching it all unfold from above. But as I stepped onto the plane, I plummeted straight back into my body, feeling every bit of heartache. Reality had well and truly hit. Just like Dorothy, I knew I had to take a deep breath and close my eyes tightly, praying I could endure the storm ahead, when all I wanted to do was to click my ruby slippers and go home – back to safety, comfort, and security. I could feel myself falling into a black hole, and I couldn't see the bottom.

What I couldn't see then but I can see clearly now is that in order for growth to occur, I had to endure discomfort. I had to be brave.

CHAPTER FOUR: DIS-EASE

If you avoid conflict to keep the peace,
you start a war inside yourself.
Cheryl Richardson

This is the part where I'm supposed to tell you how moving to the other side of the world made everything better. That our lives suddenly and miraculously changed. But of course, that wasn't the case at all. I've discovered that our outside circumstances rarely change our inner landscape.

SAME SHIT, SHINIER BUCKET

As I stepped outside into the searing hot December sun, I could feel my skin instantly tighten. The sun felt so much more ferocious than it ever did back home, and my pale English skin was suffering from the effects. I hadn't adjusted yet to the climate and found it hard to withstand the heatwave that was crippling the south of Australia. Unbeknown to us, we had arrived during one of the worst droughts on record – bloody fabulous. I was lurching from one anxiety attack to another, struggling even to venture out to buy milk at the local supermarket. The sudden realisation that we were in another country, so far from everything and everyone we knew, sent us both into a tailspin. I remember one day making a frantic call to the shipping company, ordering them to put everything back on the ship. We were going home. That was that. But, of course, we never followed through. In the words of my parents, we just 'kept on trucking'.

As I opened the taxi door and threw myself into the back seat, I nervously asked the driver if he knew where North Terrace was. He looked at me with a sympathetic smile and said, 'Yes, of course – hop in!'

I handed him the address, and off we went. I was trying to mask the terrible cough I had from a chest infection that I'd picked up on the flight over. I wasn't on my best form for a job interview, but I knew I had to 'suck it up' and get on with it. I stared blankly out of the window at a whole new world I had never seen before. Suburbia passed me by, and what seemed like an endless number of traffic lights began to heighten my anxiety about making it there on time. I ran through all of the possible questions and scenarios I would be asked and how I would cover up how sick and emotionally fragile I was. The pressure was on, and I was feeling it; we needed an income, and I wouldn't accept failure. I had never failed at an interview in my life.

Actually, that's not true. I did once, when I was just fifteen years old. I had an interview for a weekend job as a wedding photographer's assistant. Following my interview, I received a letter politely letting me down because I was too young – he wanted someone who was sixteen or over. I was gutted and felt utterly rejected. As I sat and talked it through with my dad, he said, 'If you think you can do the job, then challenge his decision. Pick up the phone and give him a call. Ask him for a trial, and if it doesn't work out, then fair enough – he can let you go.'

Despite my fear, my dad seemed to light a fire in my belly, and I thought, 'Yes, I can do this job, and I'll ask for the opportunity to prove myself'. So I called him and proposed a trial. He was so impressed with my confidence and ability to negotiate at such a young age that he couldn't say no!

And now, in these new surroundings, I once more found myself in a position where failure wasn't an option. I arrived in the city right on time. My stomach was filled with butterflies. I took some deep breaths, had a word with myself, and hurried to the elevator. I stepped out in my black patent heels, smart shirt and pencil skirt and was greeted by a pleasant receptionist.

'I'm here for an interview with Lisa,' I said.

'No problem. If you just want to take a seat, she will be with you in just a moment,' the young woman replied.

One thing I had noticed since we arrived in Australia was how completely at ease I felt around everyone I encountered. People were so welcoming; nothing was too much trouble. People would look you directly in the eye and engage with you on a level I had never felt in the UK. Why was that?

Finally, another young woman approached me, holding out her hand. 'Hi, I'm Lisa. Lovely to meet you – please come in,' she said.

She was beaming from ear to ear, and I can remember thinking she reminded me of Kylie Minogue; she was petite, beautifully dressed, and full of life. A real pocket rocket. As I sat listening to her deliver her well-practised speech about the company, their corporate values, mission statement, strategies, goals, and the like, I couldn't help but hear the whispers of my inner voice saying, 'What are you doing? You've come all the way to the other side of the world to do exactly what you've always done? This isn't your path.'

But I was in survival mode. I had to shush the voice and save it for another time. We had rent to pay, two children to feed, and a life to build, which required an income – and fast. When the interview ended, Lisa and I shook hands and she promised to get back to me later in the day with a decision.

When I arrived back at our little rental property later that afternoon, I received a phone call from the recruitment company, and I was offered the position. A sense of relief rushed over me. I felt like I could finally breathe. It was like a pressure cooker letting off steam. The 'job' box had been ticked; the 'house' box was next on the list.

And just eight weeks later, sure enough, we signed for our first home. Things were moving quickly, and although it appeared to everyone else that we were doing great with our neat little tick list complete, the reality was quite the opposite. The years of wearing the iron mask were catching up with me and I was starting to feel like I was living two separate lives. I was, as a friend once described me, a graceful swan appearing blissful as she glides through life, while her legs are waggling at a hundred miles an hour underneath. I felt uncomfortable and totally out of alignment. It started to play out in my marriage. I was struggling to cope, and eventually it all boiled over.

After a complete breakdown in our relationship, we decided to try marriage counselling. It was my first experience of any sort of talking therapy, and almost instantly I knew this was an effective way for me to deal with my emotions. To be able to pour out everything I was thinking and feeling made me feel ten stone lighter. I finally didn't feel alone, and I was no longer carrying all of this baggage around on my own. As the old BT advert put it, perfectly and simply: it's good to talk.

One day, following an hour of therapy, the counsellor looked up at me from his notepad, his pen lightly touching his lip, and gave me some advice which I have never forgotten. It would be my first 'Aha!' moment– a clear signpost along the yellow brick road.

He said, 'You must remember that you are three people in this life– you're a mother, you're a wife, and you're Kay. You seem to have forgotten about the latter.'

There's something extremely powerful about a complete stranger being able to validate what you've always sensed deep down but never dared to face. I burst into tears. For the first time, certainly in my adult life, I came to the realisation that I had completely lost myself.

Things did improve during those first few years, and life became more manageable, but it was just that: manageable. It's funny how we can have these amazing 'Aha!' moments and we arm ourselves with so much knowledge, but real change only comes when we act. As Robert Downey Jr said of his sobriety, 'It's really not that difficult to overcome these seemingly ghastly problems. What's hard is to decide to do it.'

Australia was not the answer to our problems. It wasn't the panacea we had imagined. Yes, we were living in paradise, but nothing could stop life's inevitable challenges blindsiding us, and now we didn't have the support of family and friends to help us endure the storms – we were on our own. In those first months, we were desperate for reassurance that we had done the right thing, so we'd often ask people we met from the UK if they had any regrets. I will never forget one woman we met during that time. I can still picture her clearly, standing on her front porch. She was wearing a white bikini covered with a floaty sarong, and her hair tied up neatly in a bun; I noticed how her skin was tanned and leathery from the harsh and unforgiving Australian sun. She had moved to Australia several years earlier. We had gone to look at a car she was selling – an old, beat-up Mitsubishi Magna. We were still reeling at the insane price and quietly freaking out about the cost of living since our arrival; we didn't have a lot of money behind us, and anything we did have was needed for a house deposit. After we'd politely turned down her offer, and just as we were leaving, Rick turned around and asked, 'So, was it all worth it then? You know, the move?'

She paused, then responded with, 'No regrets – but it's the same shit, just a shinier bucket.'

THERE'S NO PLACE LIKE HOME

By the end of 2008 I was still struggling to settle. I was grieving my old life. The hardest part was letting go of those we loved; life just didn't feel the same without everyone in it. I started smoking again, which I hadn't done since before the boys were born. Foolishly, I told myself it would help me to destress – not realising it was having the exact opposite effect on my body and mind. I always felt shame around smoking, starting from the first time my teacher caught me smoking at school at the age of thirteen. I can still remember smelling my nicotine-stained fingers all the way home on the school bus, hating myself, thinking what a disappointment I was to my parents. I vowed never to smoke again. But I did. The same feeling leached into my body when my dad found cigarettes in my car. He stormed into my bedroom and threw a twenty pack of Lambert & Butler on my bed. 'I take it these are yours,' he said, with just enough of an air of disgust to let me know that I was a total disappointment.

I have come to know that someone being disappointed in you is far worse and more damaging to your feelings of self-worth than someone being angry. All those years later, I still carried that underlying sense of shame around with me, hidden from sight but engraved in my veins. In that moment, though, smoking was what I saw as an easy way to cope, a distraction – an escape. I was drinking heavily, too; I didn't know it then, but my co-dependency was in full swing. To everyone else, our life looked idyllic. We both had good jobs. We had two cars, a house with a swimming pool, weekends spent at the beach, endless sunshine, amazing new friends . . . but I still had this sense of being 'out of sorts'. It niggled at me constantly. I was never willing to go deep enough to investigate it; instead I just kept packing it away in a neat little box, placing it out of sight, hoping it would go away.

By the time 2009 came around, there were major family dramas happening in the UK which resulted in disharmony and a breakdown in the relationship between my parents and my brothers. Arguments centred around the family business, money, and a struggle for control. My natural default state during any conflict is to be the peacemaker, the fixer – Pollyanna – and I was desperate to help everyone settle their differences. I couldn't bear to witness any conflict in my family, so during a visit from my parents, my dad made a desperate plea for help by offering to fly us all home for Christmas. Now, ordinarily, this would have been a wonderful idea, but I knew it was a cry for help, dressed up as a family reunion. I was about to find myself caught up in the middle of some serious 'dis-ease'.

We were due to arrive the week before Christmas to surprise the whole family. We planned it all out, telling everyone we were going away for Christmas to Kangaroo Island, a small island off the south coast of Australia. The boys could barely contain their excitement. But right from the start, the trip did not go as planned. It was the winter of 2010, which turned out to be one of the coldest winters on record in the UK, reaching temperatures of -20ºC.

We touched down at Kuala Lumpur International Airport, Malaysia, ready for our connecting flight to Manchester. As we waited in the terminal, I couldn't help but eavesdrop on the two people sitting behind us. 'It's snowing really bad over there. We might not be able to fly in – they might be closing the airport,' the young woman said to the young man sitting beside her.

Never one to be afraid to speak to any random stranger, I quickly turned around and said, 'Excuse me– did you just say the weather was really bad in England?'

'Yes. We just saw it on the news,' she said, holding her laptop up to show me the latest news report.

My heart sank. As we chatted for a few minutes, we quickly realised we were on the same flight. It turned out the young man sitting next to her was her boyfriend; they were both from Adelaide, travelling to the UK to spend Christmas with his family, just like us. We hit it off immediately. It was like we had known each other for years; we just clicked. As we boarded our next flight, we said our goodbyes and ex-changed phone numbers, planning a catch-up when we all returned to Adelaide after the festive season.

But the universe had other plans. Thirty minutes into our connecting flight, the pilot diverted due to the severe weather, and we ended up stranded in Istanbul for three days. It was a huge blow to our holiday– trapped in another coun-try, all the while eating into three days of our precious time with our family. We didn't even know if we would make it in time for Christmas Day. And not only that: just to add to our woes, Rick had been struck down with a nasty case of tonsilitis which resulted in a dash to the emergency doctor at a local hospital, where access to anyone who spoke English was limited. But, as they say, every cloud has a silver lining.

There was a rumour going around that the chief executive of Malaysian Airlines was on board, so we were all (350 of us) put up in a five-star hotel, all expenses paid by the airline. It turned out to be our very own all-inclusive holiday with our new friends from Adelaide, and it firmly cemented our friendship. I have an absolute belief in those 'meant to be' moments in life. Our friendship is still going strong twelve years later.

Eventually we landed in the UK, on 21st December 2010. It was so cold that even after twenty minutes in Dad's car with the heaters on I was still able to scratch ice with my fingernails on the inside of the windows. As I rested my head on the back seat, I watched my breath create billows of foggy air, and the jet lag started to kick in.

The three nights of boozing and subtle pulses of adrenaline in anticipation of what was coming over the next few weeks were draining me, and all I wanted to do was crawl into bed. But instead we embarked on our gruelling itinerary of catch-ups with family, friends, and old work colleagues. The entire trip ended up being a shambles. I couldn't believe how broken my family were. There was so much anger, bitterness, and resentment, and it seemed impossible to make anyone see sense. I had walked into a war zone. But the biggest shock came when I saw Syd for the first time.

We were at our parents' house for the day. Ben and Dylan and their wives had already arrived, and you could've cut the atmosphere with a knife. How had it come to this in the three years we had been gone? Then in walked a tall, overweight, sad-looking man. He looked tired, and slouched over as he stood in the archway of my parents' living room. I looked, then looked again – surely it couldn't be my little brother?

'Mummy, who's that?' Louis said, innocently.

Pausing for a moment, I replied, 'Erm . . . I'm fairly sure that's your Uncle Syd, darling.'

He was unrecognisable – even to me. I stood up and greeted him with a hug and a kiss on the cheek. His soft, podgy skin felt strange against mine. He was the complete opposite from the lean, smiley man I'd left three years earlier. He gazed straight through me. There was no feeling there; it was like a light had gone out. He stood like an empty shell.

What had happened?

After a few argumentative exchanges, everyone left, and I was dumbfounded.

But I refused to give in and was determined to try bringing everyone together again, so we organised a meal together – just me, my brothers, their wives, and a couple of close family friends. As I sat at the table watching the conversations unfold, I suddenly became very aware that I didn't recognise my own family. Were they wearing iron masks, too?

They laughed and joked as if nothing was wrong, but meanwhile our relationship as a family was in tatters. I wanted to scream at everyone, 'What are we *doing*?!' but nothing came out. I was craving authenticity, some *real* talk – but no one seemed interested. I just sat there sensing an uncomfortably large elephant in the room.

Following that meal, photos were posted on social media. The usual likes and comments were posted, except for one private message which unexpectedly arrived from Syd. It said, 'Hey Kay, there's something about this photo that bothers me. Would you please take it down? Thanks.'

Not only was the message cold and formal to me, his sister, but it confirmed for me that he was not *at ease*. Something was wrong– very wrong.

The day before we were due to fly back to the land of Oz, my parents offered to take me, Rick, and the boys out for a farewell dinner– back to the Coniston Hotel, where we went with the whole family before we left the UK for good, three years earlier. The past three weeks had been a disaster, and I was still reeling from it all. The arguments, tension and 'disease' had taken their toll and ruined what should have been a fabulous Christmas for our boys. I was clutching at straws, trying to find any positive I could, but I came up short every time.

As we sat at the large circular dining table, sipping our wine and waiting for our meal, something strange began to happen. I could no longer hear what people were saying; their voices were being sucked away into some sort of vortex circulating around me. I became light-headed and I started to feel like the floor was sinking beneath me. I was losing my bearings. Rick quickly noticed something was wrong, but I couldn't focus on his words. All I could see was his mouth moving, with no sound. All I could think was *I'm having a stroke . . . Something's wrong, I'm dying.*

The manager in charge ushered me to a hotel room, and an ambulance was called. I couldn't get my breathing under control, and I must have looked like a rabbit caught in headlights. While Dad entertained the boys, Mum and Rick stayed with me and tried to comfort me. I held my mum's hand as she kept eye contact with me, lovingly reassuring me that everything was going to be OK. I could feel a surge of emotion bubbling and I knew the tears were there, but they wouldn't come. I wouldn't let them come. I was like a volcano that had been dormant for centuries, about to wreak havoc on everything and everyone around me. It wouldn't be safe for anyone in a twenty-mile radius to come near me if that were to happen. So I kept swallowing it all down.

I was taken to the local hospital, and after a short wait in A&E and a variety of blood tests and an ECG, the doctor approached my bedside and said, 'Your blood tests are clear, Mrs Backhouse, which is good news. We can't find anything physically wrong. Have you been under any stress lately?'

My natural response was going to be, 'No, of course not. I'm fine.' But before I even had a chance to respond, Rick jumped in and said, 'Yes, yes, she has – a lot of stress,' his eyes rolling.

To which the doctor replied, 'I am fairly confident that this was a panic attack. You really must reduce your stress levels if you can.'

Oh yeah, right. And how would you suggest I do that?

We got a taxi back to my parents' house later that night, and once I had checked on the boys and knocked back a double vodka or two – for medicinal purposes, of course – I crawled into bed.

As we lifted off the next morning from Manchester Airport, I sat in my aisle seat wrestling yet another panic attack, but as soon as that seat belt sign went off and I heard the familiar 'ding-dong', I could sense the weight I'd been carrying around for the past three weeks finally lifting. Suddenly the UK wasn't our home any more. It was no longer the place I longed for or romanticised about; it had turned into a war zone that we were more than happy to leave behind. Australia had now become our safe place.

We landed safely back in Adelaide, and we had tears in our eyes as we descended the rear steps of the plane, feeling the warmth of the summer sun hit our faces. This time, these were tears of joy. As I watched Rick kneel down and kiss the tarmac, I thought, 'Now we're home'.

CHAPTER FIVE: LADY O

And the time came when the risk to remain tight
in a bud was more painful than the risk
it took to blossom.
Anais Nin

As I turned over to snooze my alarm for the third time, I wrestled with the choice between hurling my body out of bed or surrendering with a white flag. I'd had this feeling before. It wasn't just the usual Monday blues; a familiar black cloud was hanging over me, and the thought of facing anyone outside of my four walls felt so overwhelming that it would leave my palms sweaty and my heart racing. I wanted to throw up. I argued with myself.

Should I call in sick?

No, you'll be fine. Come on, snap out of it!

I hated letting people down, but today I just knew that despite my willingness to push myself, I wouldn't be able to speak to anyone without the tears falling. What I was really craving was a permission slip to release myself from the hamster wheel of society for just one day. Just enough time so I could breathe, regroup, and get myself 'back in the game'. I called work, made my excuses, and snuggled back under the duvet, feeling like I was the worst person in the world. Rick had gone to work, and the boys were at school, so I grabbed the remote and set about zoning out for the day. But as I flicked through the channels, I suddenly paused – it was *Oprah*. This had been one of my favourite shows when I was a teenager, and I would often watch it when the boys were tiny – her openness, 'real talk' and emotional dialogue with the guests on her show made my heart swell. I had always marvelled at her natural ability to connect with and understand others. As I watched the opening credits and heard the familiar music, a sudden sense of warmth came over me. It was a feeling of home. It instantly made me think of my mum and our mutual love for Ms Winfrey. *I missed my mum.* Then I heard my inner voice stirring; it whispered 'Watch it, don't turn over. It's going to make you feel better.'

Her guest on the show that day was Tom Shadyac, a Hollywood movie director most famous for the films *Ace Ventura*, *Bruce Almighty*, *Liar Liar*, and *The Nutty Professor*. My interest was immediately sparked – I had been obsessed with Jim Carrey throughout my teens and twenties. I had watched those movies so many times I could recite the scripts with ease. And it was an obsession I shared with Syd. As Tom took his seat on that famous sofa, I was surprised to hear the topic of conversation: depression and spirituality. 'What? A movie director talking about depression and spirituality? What could he be depressed about?' I thought.

As it turned out: quite a lot.

Following a bike accident, Tom had suffered a debilitating condition called post-concussion syndrome. The effects on his body and mind were so intense that he became deeply depressed, and his thoughts would eventually turn to suicide.

He was at rock bottom, and as he began to contemplate the end of his life, he wondered how he would like to spend the rest of the time he had left. As he sat talking to Oprah for the next thirty minutes or so, I could sense something shifting and stirring inside of me. Although I wasn't the famous Hollywood superstar that he was, I could relate to everything he was saying. The subject of his upcoming documentary would be 'What's wrong with the world, and what can we do about it?'. As I lay in bed that Monday afternoon, I started to wonder: what was wrong with me? And what could I do about it?

Something compelled me to immediately order his new documentary, which wasn't due out until the following January. In the meantime, I knew I needed to keep the inner momentum going. It was like the touchpaper had been lit, and I was thirsty for more. I had experienced my first conscious awakening – or what I like to call a 'remembering' – and I knew I was on to something. Like a bloodhound following a strong scent, nothing was going to stop me – and, as the old saying goes, 'when the student is ready, the teacher will appear'. I had a new-found sense of hope and excitement, and although I didn't have a name for any of it yet, I just had an overwhelming realisation that I was being guided. The scarecrow was about to find his brain.

THOUGHTS ARE OUR CURRENCY

I love the analogy that our thoughts are our currency. These words were first introduced to me at a speaking event by the respected spiritual teacher and author Dr Wayne Dyer. He describes our thoughts as our currency. He once explained that if we were to go out shopping and buy a whole bunch of stuff we didn't like – an old smelly rug, an ugly lamp, some beaten-up chairs and a broken television – we would find ourselves sitting in the house wondering why everything looked so awful. We wouldn't be happy at all. Well, it's the same with our thoughts: we should only 'purchase' the thoughts we wish to house in our minds, and evict the rest. It's often not the situation we find ourselves in that causes our suffering – it's our thoughts about it.

Up until this point, this wasn't a concept that had ever crossed my mind. I wasn't even aware of my own thoughts and the damage they were causing me. When I started to observe my thoughts more closely, I realised that many of them were negative and had left me feeling unhappy and uneasy with myself. Brendon Burchard explains this perfectly in his book *The Motivation Manifesto* when he says:

> *None of us wants to be the cause of our own*
> *failure in life – yet most often we are. It is our*
> *own inept thinking, our own bad habits that*
> *rip the vibrancy from life. We are the ultimate*
> *oppressors of our own happiness.*

I decided it was time I started being honest with myself. Let's not jump ahead too much here, though; this was a small internal awareness that I was growing and nurturing.

It wasn't like I woke up that day and suddenly my life miraculously changed. It was going to take a lot of work– years of work– and that day was just the first step, the first crack appearing in the egg that housed my true self.

I started to take inventory of my life. First up was my career. I wasn't happy in my work and hadn't been for a really long time. I was in constant denial because everyone around me told me I was really good at what I did, and the money was good. I was trapped in the invisible cage, so I truly didn't believe I was capable of doing anything else. Second on the list was my marriage. Although we were working on our issues, the same arguments kept coming up. We were stuck– nothing was changing. And finally: my family. I had been conflicted about my relationship with my family since we'd returned from our trip a few months earlier. I quite often held only resentful and angry thoughts towards them, particularly my brothers. I didn't realise it then, but the thoughts I had been creating were those of victimhood. I was in blame mode. We all were. I was convinced we would never speak to each other again, and it left me feeling empty and homesick.

It's said that we have approximately seventy thousand thoughts per day. Insane, right? Well, my thoughts would often sound like this (and still sometimes do): *That won't work– what if I lose my job? What if we can't pay the bills? I'm not good enough, I'm not pretty enough, I'm not clever enough, I don't deserve this, what if they don't like me? How could they treat me this way? Will he leave me?*

Looking back, I can see now how all of those thoughts came from a place of lack and fear. They had crept up on me by stealth, slowly infecting my mind and my Pollyanna attitude to life. I hadn't even seen it coming. None of these thoughts were coming from my true self; they came only from my false self, or what the spiritual teacher Eckhart Tolle calls our 'egoic mind'. They were thoughts full of anger, jealousy, worthlessness, and resentment. I was starting to see how my own thoughts were in fact keeping me in this endless cycle of internal suffering and unhappiness. It became clear to me that I had to start by changing my thoughts, because they were the only thing within my control.

Let me share a great analogy here which was once described by Syd. He wrote in his journal how the true self becomes lost in the false self:

> *You must see your true self as an empty coat rack.*
> *Over time more and more coats and hats are hung*
> *on this coat rack. So, you are no longer the coat*
> *rack. All of these coats and hats have been hung*
> *through old beliefs and the ego. If you are able to*
> *let go of your old beliefs and silence the ego,*
> *all of the coats and hats will fall away, allowing*
> *you to see who you truly are.*

Following the Oprah interview, I suddenly felt the urge to read. I hadn't read a book in years– probably not since I was in school. 'Why on earth did I ever stop reading?' I wondered. I jumped onto her famous book club for inspiration. I selected a few titles to get the juices flowing: *The Secret* by Rhonda Byrne, and *A New Earth* by Eckhart Tolle. When they arrived a week or so later, it was like a sudden rush of childhood memories flooding back in as I collected them from the mailbox. As I held the books in my hands, I felt that same connection I had felt when I held books as a child – it was a sense of being grounded. They plugged me back into myself somehow. I flicked through the pages, holding them up to inhale the fresh smell of the print.

I started reading that very same day. It reignited my passion for literature. I read in bed, on the train, in waiting rooms, during my lunch break, on the beach– anywhere I could. My mind became open, unlocked. For the first time in my adult life, I felt liberated. I suddenly felt like I had some control over my life again – both my hands were back on the steering wheel.

A MAGICAL LUNCH

I arrived early– my usual style. I had arranged to meet a client for lunch– let's call him Ben– to say thank you for a recent placement I'd made on his team. I had been recruiting medical sales reps for a number of pharmaceutical and device companies for the past three years and had discovered I was pretty bloody good at it. But being good at something and enjoying it are two very different things. I was yearning for meaning and purpose in my work. I wanted to be of service to others in some way, but this wasn't it. Since the Oprah show, I had been practising applying my new-found knowledge; I was changing my thoughts gradually, but it often felt like I was going two steps forward and three steps back. Anyone who's tried it will know that changing old habits is extremely difficult. As the author Anne Lamott says in her book of the same name, 'you have to take it bird by bird'. I had lost my passion for my work, so in order for me to keep functioning and dragging myself there every day, I had to take my focus away from everything I hated and shift it to everything I loved and wanted to welcome into my life. What I was practising was the law of attraction. I put my faith in the universe and stayed open-minded. I would often sit on the train practising manifesting techniques that I learnt from Tony Robbins's brilliant book, *Unlimited Power*. Yes, I became the strange woman who sat on the train staring at the floor, trying to manifest my future! Joking aside, though, I genuinely started to believe I could change my own path. And gradually, things really did start to change.

As we ordered a couple of glasses of tasty Sauvignon Blanc with our lunch (standard in Australia), we started with a bit of small talk about the weather and what our plans were for the weekend. Ben and I had only met on a couple of occasions, but we had hit it off straight away. We had a similar sense of humour, and his kind and caring nature was obvious from the outset, with his focus always on the wellbeing of his team.

Not long into the conversation, he paused, glanced up from his lunch with a quizzical look and asked, 'So tell me,

Kay. Recruitment must be a really tough gig. How long have you been doing it for? Surely you don't want to do it forever?'

'Thirteen years,' I quickly replied, always the proud martyr. 'It certainly takes a certain type of person to do it.' Then I paused before saying, 'If I can be brutally honest with you, I'm not sure if I'm that person any more.'

I think he could sense the uneasy level of vulnerability in my response. Was this the universe answering me? I could tell his question was genuine, so I followed my instincts and took the opportunity to drop the iron mask, open up and speak honestly. I didn't have anything to lose.

People often come into your life at just the right time, and this was one of those occasions. What started out as a thank you lunch turned out to be a career coaching session and an invitation to interview for a medical sales rep position in Ben's team, later that year. I couldn't believe what was happening. I didn't have a nursing qualification – a normal prerequisite for these positions – and I had zero experience. It was unheard of for someone with my background to even be considered for the position. I had no other conclusion other than the universe had answered my call.

When the job was advertised around early September, I applied immediately, but it wasn't a quick process. After attending my initial interview, I was called back twice more: once to give a sales presentation, and the second time to be grilled by the national sales director. What I didn't realise at the time was that Ben was fighting with head office to hire me; it turned out the human resources department didn't believe I was the right fit based on my CV and were pushing for another candidate. But Ben was relentless, never giving in, believing in his own inner voice that I was the right person for the role – and at the beginning of October 2011, I finally got the job. I was ecstatic.

My life changed overnight. I resigned from my thirteen-year recruitment career and excitedly joined the world of medical sales. I suddenly realised I was capable of so much more, and all because I'd changed my thoughts and become open to what the universe had to offer, and someone believed in me. The stars had aligned.

LABELS

*I simply feel that a human being must always
recognise that he is qualitatively more than any
system of thought he can imagine,
and therefore he should never label himself.
He degrades himself when he does.*
Alan Watts

I've never liked the word 'depression'. Even the word is . . . well, depressing. Being labelled a depressed person can be problematic. It's a risky game we play when we stick labels on the heads of others. It's often that label that can pigeonhole an individual, which in turn can perpetuate the stigma and the cycle of low mental health, keeping them trapped in their false beliefs and old conditioning. I find this is rife with labels like 'addict' and 'autistic' – they're all just labels, and they do not define that person. We mean well when we use them, but they are far too generalised and don't tell an individual's story. Human beings are not a number; we are real people with real and varied stories. Such labels can also give the perception that a person is 'wrong' or 'not normal', leading to a sense of shame and separation.

The truth is, our human mind wants and needs to label everything. It's the only way it can make sense of the world. We take in so much information at incredible speed that we need to compartmentalise it somehow, and we often use labels to do that. It's our way of making sense out of chaos. Essentially, I have found that labels often allow the ego to grow while forcing the soul to shrink.

So what's wrong with using labels? Well, nothing, in theory – the problems only seem to arise when we're unconscious of these labels. Then they can become restrictive and oppressive and cause us to put ourselves, and each other, into neatly labelled boxes. Without conscious awareness, they become the lies we tell ourselves, and we remain locked in the invisible cage. For example, 'I'm not creative' was something I had told myself, a self-limiting belief – a label I had adopted from an early age. Why? Because I was an average student in my art class. I couldn't draw or paint. No one ever explained to me that creativity doesn't just reside in the end of a pencil or a paintbrush. So a false belief grew inside of me, and the more I repeated it in my mind, the more I believed it.

I loved writing poetry when I was a teenager, but stopped when I was repeatedly teased by the other kids at school. I loved reading, but I stopped because my friends labelled me boring. I loved dancing when I was a child, but I gave it up when I went to high school and traded it in for smoking and drinking with my mates on the weekends. What a waste.

I have vivid memories of recounting the steps to a tap dance routine, as I launched myself with vigour around the village hall in my green-and-white striped leotard while my mum proudly watched on. I didn't have a name for how I felt when I danced back in 1986, but now I would call it 'connected' – I was in alignment with my authentic and impersonal self. It's similar to how my daily yoga practice makes me feel now. But at the time, I didn't know any of those things were creative; I just thought they were fun – the kinds of things you get to do when you're a child, but leave behind when you grow up, get a job, get married, buy a house, have children, and live happily ever after with your Prince Charming. What a tragedy that I should spend the next thirty or so years of my life believing I wasn't creative!

I AM

I AM – two simple words. For me, in 2012, they became two of the most significant words to enter my consciousness. *I Am* was the title of a documentary by Tom Shadyac. Ever since the moment I watched his interview on *Oprah* ten months prior, I had witnessed my life beginning to change, and I had an intense knowing that this documentary was about to take me a little further along my 'yellow brick road'. The Tin Man was about to find his heart.

As I settled down on the sofa to enjoy the first screening, I heard the opening music start: 'Where Is The Love' by the Black-Eyed Peas. Such a powerful song, with poignant lyrics. Those words instantly moved me, and within the first five minutes I could feel goosebumps from head to toe, a surge of energy heaving in my chest, and my eyes welled up. What was this feeling I was experiencing?

The film turned out to be a never-ending flurry of 'Aha!' moments. I felt like someone who had been suffering with amnesia and all of a sudden I was remembering my old life for the first time. There was one clear message during those seventy-eight minutes: each of us is an intrinsic part of nature, and our separation as human beings is just an illusion, and it's that illusion of separation that's making us sick. Then it dawned on me; could the reason I had been feeling so depressed be because society was set up in such a way that it was pushing me to compete and consume when my true nature was screaming at me to cooperate and care? One trait leads to disconnection with the true self, but the other leads to connection.

I received the message loud and clear that day. All I had to do was listen to my true self and follow the rhythm of nature. I felt utterly inspired, or as Dr Wayne Dyer would say, 'in-spirit'. I suddenly had a renewed sense of hope – for life, for other human beings, for the world, and for me.

CHAPTER SIX: THE 'C' WORD

Few words are as emotionally charged
as the word cancer.
Travis Christofferson MS

For most of my early life, the word 'cancer' wasn't one I feared. It happens to be my star sign, the sign of the crab. I had only ever associated the word with talk of my personality as a deeply sensitive, emotional homebody and what my husband would refer to as the crab that was 'stuck under her rock'. But in 1998 the word took on a whole new meaning when my grandad, known fondly to the family as 'Ganky', was diagnosed with bowel cancer. It was unexpected. He hadn't complained about feeling unwell, and we hadn't noticed any changes in him – but as symptoms arose that he could no longer ignore, a doctor's visit was arranged. I can recall walking into the kitchen as my mum got off the phone with my Gran.

'It's bowel cancer,' she said calmly.

'So what does that mean?' I replied.

She explained how the hospital was proposing surgery to remove the cancer, and hopefully that would be that.

'Phew!' I thought. I had heard a lot about people getting cancer and recovering – going into remission. Of course, I knew some didn't survive, but that wouldn't be my Ganky.

He would be fine. He was strong as an ox.

I was eighteen at the time, and my life was mostly taken up with a new job I'd started in July of that year, and going out, getting drunk and dabbling in drugs most weekends. Then one weekend in mid August, following one of my regular bust-ups with my boyfriend, I decided to take a drive over to see Ganky. It would be just the tonic I needed – a safe, happy place to shelter me from the storm.

It was a Sunday afternoon – always my favourite day to be at my grandparents' house. Growing up, it's where we went most weekends. Gran would always be cooking something delicious in the kitchen. It was a hive of activity with the pressure cooker squealing, the Kenwood mixer whirring and the breeze blowing through the back door, whipping up the multicoloured plastic fly screen. Every now and again she would pause, standing in her flowery apron with sweat beading from her brow, to take a sip of her customary can of lager before she got right back to it. It was what I call 'organised chaos'. And I loved it.

As I rang the doorbell, I took a deep breath in and let out a huge sigh, trying to push away my hangover and all of the upset from the day before. They had moved to a new flat after downsizing the previous year, so I was still getting used to their new surroundings. It was no longer the house that held all our childhood memories, but somehow they still managed to make it feel just as warm and inviting. Gran had this natural skill of making you feel like you were the most special person in the world whenever you visited. They were both well known for being fantastic hosts, with a never-ending flow of food and drink from the moment you stepped in. Nothing was ever too much trouble.

However, on this particular day, it all felt vastly different. As I climbed the stairs and walked into the living room, I could see Ganky was sitting in his chair. I noticed he was more subdued than normal, but that didn't stop him beaming at me across the room. He rose up from his chair and greeted me with a big bear hug.

'Ah, it's my Katie Kitten,' he said proudly. It was a nickname he'd given me as a child, and I never, ever got sick of him calling me that. It always made me feel special, and stirred up memories of staring at him through my six-year-old eyes, sitting on his knee as he told me stories late into the afternoon. He was an incredible storyteller.

This day felt different. The first thing I noticed was that he was in his dressing gown. It was the middle of the day and this was unheard of for him – he was from a generation of men who would dress in well-pressed shirts and trousers at all times, and quite often a paisley tie, complete with a big fat Windsor knot. As we sat there chatting for a while, I couldn't help but notice a book on the arm of his chair, which he had obviously been reading before I'd arrived. It was a book about death.

I felt myself instantly recoil. I don't recall the title of the book, but what I do remember is that it was a spiritual book, full of talk about angels and heaven. It was a book to help someone prepare for their own death. As we fumbled a few awkward words about it, I picked it up and flicked through the pages, pretending I was interested. I can remember a rush of adrenaline and the panic rising in my body. *No, no, no! He can't die!* I screamed inside. *If he just puts the book away, then no one ever needs to know about it, and it will all go away.*

Isn't it funny how we believe that if we don't talk about something, it won't happen? Death has become so taboo in our society that this is often how we deal with it. We try to hide it, pretend it doesn't exist, when in reality it is as natural as birth and everything in between. As Rick said to me recently, 'The two things we can most definitely be sure of in this life are birth and death.' We have to change this perception of death. (There's more on this in Part Three.)

Even though no one had directly told me, it was clear that Ganky's prognosis wasn't good. As I got up to leave, we hugged. I was fighting to hold back my tears, not knowing which ones were for him and which were for the shitty mess my life was in. He thrust a five-pound note into my hand and said, 'Here, go treat yourself. Get yourself out with your friends and have a drink on me.' Although we never talked about it, he could tell I wasn't happy in my life at that time; all it took was a knowing glance as I left, which said it all.

The cancer had spread from his bowel to his liver, and just three weeks later – only six weeks after the original diagnosis – my precious Ganky died. He was seventy-two years old. It all happened so quickly I hardly had a chance to process what was going on. Cancer had become my enemy number one overnight, and it wasn't a word I wanted to hear about ever again.

BIRTHDAY

The first time Syd noticed something was physically wrong was on his wedding night in June 2008. He would explain to me that he'd felt a searing, burning, intense pain running up and down his spine which resulted in him lying on the bathroom floor of his hotel room in the middle of the night, writhing around in agony. Of course, he told no one – not even his new wife.

I'm trying not to generalise here, but I think most people would agree that men struggle to openly discuss how they're feeling and will often hide pain – both emotional and physical. Some will go months, even years, until something gets so bad that they have no choice but to see a doctor, by which time the damage has already been done. Syd was no different, except he had the added layer of a 'never give in' attitude to life which, although in many ways an admirable trait, also caused him to be awfully stubborn at times. As with many of us, he was often at the root of his own suffering.

After that night, despite his fear about the intensity of pain he had experienced, he carried on as normal and didn't tell another soul. He would later tell me that he believed the pain he experienced was his body's reaction to his emotional unease about the direction his life was taking. He felt he had made all the wrong choices from the age of twenty-one and was trapped in a life that wasn't meant for him. The train had left the station, and he couldn't see a way of getting off.

Syd and I had grown apart after Rick and I emigrated. It's natural for siblings to grow apart during the different phases of life, and we were no different. However, despite the distance, our parallel lives continued; we were both living lives that were not aligned to our true selves.

On the surface, things were rosy: we were both 'happily' married, with children, careers, and lovely homes. But at the core, we were both desperately unhappy and looking for an escape hatch. Remember in Chapter Four how I said I knew something was very wrong during our trip to the UK? Well, my fears were later confirmed. After almost three years of his body trying to speak to him but being ignored, it finally screamed at him in January of 2011. He went to see the local GP in March with a smorgasbord of symptoms: depression, severe back pain with reduced mobility, muscle weakness, unexplained stretch marks all over his body, swelling, weight gain, high blood pressure, memory loss, and poor sleep patterns. You name it, he had it. MRI scans and a plethora of blood tests were performed at Airedale Hospital and then St James's Hospital in Leeds, and they would reveal his first diagnosis: he had Cushing's disease.

I had never heard of it before, and set about researching it immediately. Cushing's disease is a condition in which your body is producing and releasing too much cortisol (the stress hormone) into the body. Over time, this causes your body to effectively disintegrate from the inside out. The problem in Syd's case was that we didn't know what was causing it, so the next step was to find out.

First up was an MRI scan of his brain. This would reveal a small lump on his pituitary gland, but as written in his doctor's notes, it was thought to be a 'red herring'. Then on his twenty-eighth birthday – 1st September 2011 – he received the news that in fact, the cause of his Cushing's disease was cancer. To be exact, a neuroendocrine carcinoma of the thymus. It was the size of two golf balls, and it was buried deep in his chest cavity.

As I put the phone down, my blood ran cold. I looked at Rick and said in disbelief, 'Syd's got cancer.'

At this stage I didn't know any other details, but the details didn't matter – he had *cancer*. In my mind, all I really heard was: 'Syd's going to die'. Cancer and death to me went hand in hand. My thoughts went immediately back to 1998 and watching my Ganky take his final breaths. My mind also became flooded with thoughts of celebrities who'd passed away in recent years from cancer. In 2009 Jade Goody, a young mum of two, died from cervical cancer. I didn't know her personally, of course, but she was someone the whole country had come to know from the reality show *Big Brother*. Her entire cancer journey – even her funeral– was televised for the whole world to see. The whole thing was heartbreaking and, for me, overwhelming. The very same year, my teenage heartthrob Patrick Swayze died from pancreatic cancer. I would often wonder how it was possible for this big, strong, powerful beast of a man to effectively shrivel up and die in a matter of just a few years. Being the empath that I am, these deaths caused me not only to feel a genuine sense of grief, but also to be able to sense their fear. It became my fear. It haunted me. Seeing these people go from healthy, thriving individuals to empty shells was hard to get my head around.

My knowledge of cancer at the time was, at best, basic. All I knew was the statistic from the TV ads: one in three (eventually becoming one in two) people would get cancer in their lifetime. I never really believed that statistic, though – it seemed absurd that this could be happening to so many but that, with all the technological advances happening around the world, we weren't able to fix it. I certainly never thought it would happen to anyone else in our family – and least of all that it would happen to my little brother.

During all of this, I was still on the other side of the world from my entire family. So not only was the news devastating, but I also immediately felt trapped. I had no way out. I knew I couldn't fly home – and even if I did, what use would I be? I was smack bang in the middle of the interview process for the medical sales job, we didn't have any savings, and at that time the idea of leaving Rick and the boys to fly home on my own sent my anxiety into overdrive. It was unimaginable. So my thoughts turned instead to 'What can I do to help?' – I had to keep focused and feel useful. I needed to turn this sense of helplessness into something productive.

I would sit at the computer night after night, researching everything I could about neuroendocrine cancer. I found myself falling down a rabbit hole, uncovering what felt like endless amounts of information – not ideal for an overthinker. It helped me that I already had some understanding and knowledge of medical terminology from my time working in medical recruitment. It helped me to sift the wheat from the chaff and gave me the confidence to pick up the phone to specialists all over the world and start asking questions. I would report back to my parents in the UK on all my findings and arm them with questions to take to Syd's appointments. I had to become his voice. My parents and I had become his advocates overnight, and it didn't matter what side of the world I was on. My mission was clear and simple: I had to save his life. A letter from the local GP to the specialists in Leeds in October 2011 expressing our frustrations around their lack of urgency following Syd's diagnosis would demonstrate our fighting spirit early on:

> *One of the main things the family is bothered about is that Syd has a serious medical condition which is life-threatening (his sister has done some internet searches and so they are now fully aware of the likely ten-year survival rate with this condition) but they only found out about the condition because we asked for faxes of the histology report to be sent through . . . I really think Syd and his family will go apoplectic if he is not informed before [date] about what the problem is and what the likely treatment plan is.*

Our fight to get things moving finally worked, and two weeks later, Syd underwent complex cardiothoracic surgery at St James's Hospital. It was a seven-hour operation in which they opened up his entire chest cavity and removed the tumour, which was inconveniently nestled right next to his heart. We were told later that it had infiltrated into the delicate membrane around his heart. This meant they were not able to remove all of the cancerous cells, so there was a chance that the cancer could return at some stage in the future.

In some ways, dealing with cancer was the easy part; the immediate – and what would turn out to be ongoing – challenges related to what the overproduction of cortisol had done to Syd's body during his years without a diagnosis. It had caused four of his vertebrae to fracture and collapse – resulting in a four-inch height loss – and he was diagnosed with osteoporosis. His skin had turned into tissue paper and he was at constant risk of skin tears. Effectively, he was a twenty-eight-year-old man in a ninety-year-old's body. This cascade of hormones pumping through his body had also brought about a severe bout of depression. His mental health had deteriorated – and he would later tell me, with tears in his eyes, of his wish to end it all during that time. He would try to make light of it by joking that the only reason he hadn't jumped from the window was that he couldn't get out of his wheelchair. Even as I write this now, I can still be transported back in time to the moment he sat on the sofa in my living room in Australia, describing the horrific physical and mental trauma he sustained during those months. I knew it had damaged him. This wasn't just about a wound in his chest; he had a wound in his soul.

FALLING APART

After Syd's operation, there was a sense of just slipping back into normal life as though nothing had really happened. By January 2012 he was feeling really good – his cortisol levels had returned to normal since the tumour had been removed, and he was slowly rebuilding his strength. Following his divorce in 2011, he had even met someone he would later describe as the girl of his dreams – Emily. He spent 2012 experiencing utter bliss, telling me it was one of the happiest times of his life. He felt renewed and had been given another lease of life. Our relationship had changed, too, and we were back to speaking on the phone semi-regularly, keeping up to date with his progress. We started to feel much closer.

Meanwhile, my home life had become very busy. We had built and moved into a beautiful new home (the first of two), and my new job was flying me all over the country, meeting new people and enjoying new experiences – but the underlying issues remained the same. I was still unhappy, still drinking excessively, and still trying to 'fix' my husband. How could I feel this sense of loneliness when my life was so full?

Despite all the self-help books I had read and the 'Aha!' moments I'd experienced, nothing much had changed. My conditioned mind was still stuck in an endless loop of 'Why me? Why us? How could they?'. As far as I was concerned, life was happening to me and I was the victim. I was suffering, and my default position was always to go around trying to fix everything and everyone else outside of myself – if I could do that, then I'd feel better, right? Wrong.

By early 2013 we had moved to the countryside to build another home – still searching outside of ourselves for our happy place. Rick's mental health was taking another downward spiral. It's difficult to explain what it's like to live with someone who is constantly battling mental illness. I always felt at the mercy of whatever he was feeling and had this overwhelming feeling of responsibility to hold it all together. Physically he was there, but emotionally he was often AWOL. Then in May of that very same year, my body decided it couldn't carry the load any more.

It was Mother's Day and we had been out for a meal to celebrate with the boys, just the four of us. Something felt wrong. I had intense pain in my lower back, causing me to limp. Although I'd suffered with some low-level back pain since giving birth to the boys, this felt different. I hadn't fallen or injured myself in any way; it just seemed to appear from nowhere. I brushed it off as just the result of sleeping in a bad position the night before.

The next morning, I awoke early and headed off to the airport for a work trip to Darwin, in the Northern Territory. It was a three-hour flight and by the time I landed, my back was getting worse. I spent the next five days popping a cocktail of painkillers just so I could get from my hotel to the local hospital where I was working. My 'never quit' attitude kicked in – I was determined to keep going and get the job done – but the thought of attempting to get on a flight home was starting to weigh on my mind. My mobility had become so bad that I was having to lift my legs in and out of the car one at a time using my hands. The pain was excruciating. I would phone Rick at night from my hotel room in tears. Despite his efforts to get me to fly home early, I refused. I would explain how important that week was, and that I couldn't let my customers or my team down. I was stubborn, just like my brother.

I eventually flew home on Friday, barely able to move, sitting like a statue in my seat. I have no memory of leaving the plane or how I made it to my car; all I can remember is pulling into the driveway and making a calm but desperate call to Rick asking him to come and meet me outside. Frozen in the driver's seat, I couldn't move. It was as if my body had held on when it had to but now it knew I was home, it just gave up.

Rick looked at me, horrified. 'Oh my God, why didn't you tell me it was this bad?'

I couldn't hold back the tears as he lovingly scooped me up and lifted me gently out of the car. He carried me into the house and laid me on the bed and, without any argument from me, he called an ambulance.

It turned out I had been walking around with a herniated disc for over a week, and because of my stubbornness I had made it worse than it needed to be. The next three months involved hospital admissions, MRI scans, blood tests, physiotherapy, and a number of complications from my pain medications. In addition, I received a new diagnosis. I was suffering with a condition called ankylosing spondylitis – a disease which, over time, can cause the spine to fuse together like a stick and, in the worst cases, confine people to a wheelchair. It was a disease my dad had suffered with since his early twenties. It turned out I carried the same faulty gene, and the doctors confirmed I was symptomatic. It was the first time in my life that I was completely debilitated. I was out of action, and no amount of positive thinking or wishing things to be different was going to change my situation. I had to sit with it. I had no other choice but to focus on how I could get through this mentally, so I decided to start journaling.

I hadn't written anything down since I was a teenager, but the whisper of my inner voice returned and told me it was the right thing to do. I picked up a journal my mum had given me years earlier. On the front page, it read:

> *This book is full of my love for you, so whenever you need me, just fill its pages with your own words. I will always be here. All my love Mum.*

Her words would speak to my inner voice, and I could feel her love through the pages. I needed her more than she would ever know.

I began unpacking my thoughts. I wrote regularly for those few months, and looking back I can see how it really helped me to start making sense of my thoughts and feelings. I suddenly started to become the observer of my life, rather than a helpless passenger. My internal narrative changed from 'Why is this happening to me?' to 'What is this teaching me?'. I was becoming a seer rather than a seeker. It was a small but profound change. Anyone who has experienced a debilitating health condition will know that you very quickly become grateful for what can often feel like trivial things. I began practising gratitude every day.

During my rehabilitation, I attended hydrotherapy sessions at the local swimming pool. As I shuffled along the side of the pool on my walking frame and cautiously dipped my toe in the water to test the temperature, I can remember thinking 'I don't belong here with all of these old people'. I was the only person under the age of seventy. I was embarrassed, even ashamed, at the fact that my body had let me down, and I instinctively knew it was my own fault.

Now, I need to point out here that I have been blessed with a high metabolism since birth. It runs in our family. I was the one that everyone hated because I could eat what I wanted without putting on an ounce of weight. I only had to stand up and I'd lose five hundred calories. But I was beginning to feel like what I would call a 'skinny fat person' – on the outside I looked slim, fit and healthy, but on the inside I was fat and unhealthy. I hadn't exercised regularly in any form since I was at school. This was now starting to come back and bite me. I had absolutely no core strength. One thing was clear: since Syd's cancer diagnosis two years prior, I had been forced into an uncomfortable awareness of how much I'd neglected my body over the years, and now my own physical illness prompted me to focus on doing something about it. I made a promise to myself there and then that I would start to exercise regularly.

The physiotherapist and doctors had told me I needed to strengthen my core to better support my back, hopefully reducing the risk of my disc herniating again in the future. And I knew I somehow had to reduce my chance of ending up in a wheelchair – that was not even up for negotiation.

After a few weeks of feeling sorry for myself, I decided dwelling on my diagnosis was not the answer – so I turned my thoughts to how I could heal myself. One book I read during that time – *All is Well*, by Louise Hay – really opened my eyes to the mind–body connection and its potential for healing. Louise discusses how we can use the body's own intuition to heal ourselves from physical symptoms brought on by our imbalanced emotions. I had never heard anyone discuss this subject before, and yet instantly it seemed I knew that what she was trying to convey was true. As I eagerly absorbed the book, nodding, agreeing with her every word, one thing stood out: any disease or imbalance related to the back indicated feelings of being unsupported in the world. It was another lightbulb moment. She had hit the nail on the head. I felt completely unsupported and lost. In addition, she went on to say that arthritis represented feelings of being unloved, along with criticism and resentment. My body was trying to teach me something, and for the first time in my life I felt empowered to take responsibility for my own recovery.

By early August I was finally able to return to work. It had been three months, and although nervous and apprehensive, I knew I needed to get back to normal life and be around other humans again. I committed to my new 'getting healthy' programme and started an 'at home' exercise regime. For years I had tried to force myself to go to the gym (because that's what everybody else did), but I failed to stick at it. I would tell myself it was just a lack of determination, that I was pathetic – but when I really started to look at it, I realised I didn't enjoy any part of the experience, so why did I keep insisting on trying to fit a round peg into a square hole? Driving there after work, the changing rooms, the smell of everyone's sweaty bodies, everyone staring at me as I fumbled, trying to navigate the machinery. I felt like I was in a goldfish bowl. It felt awkward, and I hated every minute of it. It had never occurred to me that there were other ways of getting fit, and it was possible to find something that was better suited to me. I needed something I could do in the comfort of my own home, without equipment. After a recommendation from a psychotherapist I was seeing at the time, I found Kayla Itsines and her Bikini Body Guide (a programme that has since been renamed to Sweat). If you don't know her work, she's a young woman from Adelaide, South Australia who focuses on making it possible to exercise for just twenty-eight minutes each day without equipment. She's followed by millions on her social media pages, and what really gelled with me was her holistic approach to being healthy and living a life of balance. It wasn't just about a healthy body; she focused on overall wellbeing. For me, it was perfect. I knew it was something I could stick to, so I signed up immediately.

I saw changes in my body within just a couple of months, recording my progress on my phone. I started to feel better in both body and mind and suddenly found the motivation to begin taking regular walks in addition to the programme. I was making some positive changes, but I felt they were just small steps; I was still very much aware that I was drinking heavily, still needed to tackle my diet and I was yet to fully explore my emotional baggage.

In hindsight I can see I was putting a lot of unnecessary pressure on myself, which in many ways started to work against me. I wanted to achieve it all overnight. I was unrealistic in my expectations of myself and would feel overwhelmed at the mountain of steps I still had to climb. I would often feel like a failure if I couldn't get it right the first time. I was never comfortable being a work in progress. In other words, I was suffering from the disease of perfectionism. I became stuck and unmotivated.

A phone call would change all of that.

In September I received the call I'd convinced myself I would never receive: Syd's cancer had come back. A routine scan had revealed that those annoying cells around his heart which the surgeons had to leave behind during his original surgery had spread from his chest to his lymph nodes. I was frozen as I held the phone to my ear, trying to take in what my mum was saying. My immediate reaction was to find out what treatment the doctors could offer and how quickly they could do it. I had entered panic mode, but I sat and listened intently as she explained that surgery wasn't an option. There was some chemotherapy on offer; however, the chances of it being effective were limited. The reality was, this was such a rare cancer that it left even the best specialists scratching their heads, wondering what to do. He was one in five million. They had little clinical data to support the effectiveness of any treatments. I put the phone down and rose quietly from my seat.

My memory is blank after that, but Louis told me in later years that he watched me get up from my seat at the table, walk out of the back door and proceed to walk laps of our rented two-acre property continuously for about half an hour in a complete daze. As the boys got up to follow me, Rick calmy whispered to them, 'Just let her walk.'

A few weeks later Syd decided to start chemotherapy, but after one session he stopped, admitting to me that the only reason he'd agreed to it was his feeling of guilt around letting everyone down. He said he didn't want everyone to think he wasn't trying to save himself – he just instinctively knew that injecting a poisonous substance (which nurses were not even allowed to touch without wearing gloves) into his veins was not the answer. He felt it didn't make any logical sense. Not only that; it also only had a ten per cent chance of working, a statistic that he felt wasn't worth the reduced quality of life he would have to endure. Of course, we wholeheartedly supported his decision, but naturally our conversations then turned to 'What now?'.

PART TWO

AWAKENING

CHAPTER SEVEN: THE VISIT

Life is really simple,
but we insist on making it complicated.
Confucius

In the final months of 2013, after declining chemotherapy, my little brother was handed a prognosis of just two years. For me, this was utterly unpalatable. He was just thirty years old. As I struggled to grapple with the idea of a world without him in it, I just couldn't understand why he wasn't being offered the usual multitude of treatments like everybody else. Why was he so different?

The harsh truth was that hardly anyone knew anything about neuroendocrine cancer. It wasn't one of the common cancers like breast cancer, bowel cancer, lung cancer and prostate cancer. It wasn't plastered all over the mainstream media. There were no televised fundraisers or GoFundMe pages for this elusive creature. Unless you went looking for it, you would never know it even existed. In fact, it was so unknown and unpopular that when Steve Jobs succumbed to cancer in 2011, it was only ever described in the media as pancreatic cancer, which was false; he died from neuroendocrine cancer of the pancreas.

There was also little awareness or knowledge about it among the medical professionals. With just a tiny fraction of the population suffering from this disease, little focus was given to it in terms of funding and research, which meant there was scant evidence for any effective treatments. The reality was it wasn't a cool, sexy cancer. There was no spotlight. Syd was left in the dark, abandoned. In his own words, he was 'left to rot'. He felt like the doctors had washed their hands of him, and he had no choice other than to fend for himself.

'Isn't there anything else they can do?' I would plead. I just couldn't get my head around the fact that they would effectively give up on him like that. Surely there must be other specialists around the world who had more knowledge of his disease? I had heard of people flying to other countries for innovative cancer treatments – why weren't we being offered the same? There must be someone who could help us. My mind was whirring with questions, and I wasn't just going to let it go, but I sensed that for the time being the conversations needed to shift gears. So my parents sat down with him and had the conversation nobody wants to have with their child.

'What do you want to do with the time you have left?' they asked.

His first response was, 'I want to go and see my sister in Australia. Let's fly business class.'

And so, two months later, that's exactly what they did.

PEAS AND CARROTS

It was summer in Australia, and we were moving into the new home we had just finished building in the barren countryside. We were cutting it fine, but managed to move

115

in just a few weeks before my brother's arrival.

I can remember feeling nervous and apprehensive about the visit. We hadn't seen each other since that awful Christmas in 2010, and although his cancer diagnosis had broken the silence between us, we'd only had brief conversations over the phone. Not only that, but we hadn't lived under the same roof since we were kids, and I could feel the pressure mounting. Was it going to be awkward? What would we talk about? How different would he look? Would he talk about his cancer? Would we all get along for three whole weeks?

But something strange and magical happened as soon as he stepped into my car at the airport that warm February day. We both felt an immediate connection and sense of ease, and suddenly all my worries melted away. It was as if all those years of hurt and upset had never even happened; they just disappeared into the abyss. I can't remember exactly what we talked about in the car for the next hour or so, but I do remember that our conversation flowed in perfect motion like two synchronised swimmers. It felt so natural. And just like Forrest Gump and Jenny, we were like kids again, back to being just like peas and carrots. That was us – peas and carrots. And that's how we would stay from that moment forward.

BOTTLE OF RED

That first night together, we stood in the kitchen, huddled around the breakfast bar, blanketed in the lingering 'new house' smell. We talked, laughed, and drank champagne until the early hours of the morning. My parents were floating in a haze of jet lag, the boys were still in an adrenaline rush of excitement, and Syd was still on cloud nine from his business class flight. I could see he was in total awe and amazement of Australia and our new home. He had only ever imagined our life in Oz; he'd never seen it up close and personal. I could tell he was inspired.

As the night continued, I glanced from time to time at Rick. I could see that he was lovingly watching on as I took mental photos. I was hanging on to every word uttered and savouring every moment as if it were my last. I had become totally unaware of the time of day, and it simply did not matter. There were no rules any more. It was like time stood still. I was living in the now.

Something unusual happens when someone receives a terminal diagnosis. It's as if the lens of their life comes into sharp focus – life suddenly gets very real, very simple, very quickly. And through my own personal experience, I've found that this doesn't just apply to the person with the terminal illness; it's also relevant to those closest to them. What I didn't realise at the time was that my highly sensitive soul, coupled with the deep connection I had with my brother, would catapult me to living and breathing every moment with him. I was fast becoming an extension of him. Whatever he felt, I felt, and vice versa. We would later call this our 'twin syndrome'.

We spent those first few days together visiting the local wineries and beautiful beaches, and enjoying the simple pleasures of eating good food, drinking fine wine, and watching our favourite movies together. Eventually, though, our topics of discussion became much deeper. One particular day that sticks in my mind was when we spent the evening having dinner with my boss and his wife, who happened to be our neighbours. They put on a delicious feast for us, and as conversations flowed around the dinner table, Syd turned to look at me and without hesitation said, 'Do you think you will ever come back home?'

I was caught off guard and wasn't really ready to answer the question, so I shot a response back at him that I now know came from my false self. 'Not a chance. Why would I leave here and go back to that load of bullshit?'

As much as I wanted to believe that things could be better among my family, I had little faith at that time. As a form of survival, my brain had formed pathways over those years of repetitive hate for the UK, purely based on that one Christmas. How powerful our thoughts can be! I had become so attached to a story I'd been telling myself that I had unknowingly estranged myself from everyone and everything I had once loved. I was angry and resentful, and it had become easier to live my life where the UK became 'out of sight, out of mind'. I now lived in a beautiful country, with amazing friends and a job I loved. The reality was, I had become distracted – that was, until Syd's questions started to shine a light on everything I had been avoiding. It was right there, in my face.

Unbeknown to me at the time, he was subtly leaving breadcrumbs so I would find my way home. One such breadcrumb was a bottle of wine he purchased at our favourite winery, The Winehouse, in a tiny little place called Langhorne Creek in South Australia. It was a bottle of 2009 John's Blend Shiraz; I remember it well because it was an expensive bottle, an elixir to those who appreciate a good bottle of red. This may not seem significant – but Syd wasn't a drinker. He would have the occasional glass of wine, but he never enjoyed the effect alcohol had on him, so would always keep it limited. So when he picked up this bottle of wine, I was surprised. At first I thought he was going to give it to Rick as a gift, but then he told me that he was taking it home. I looked at him, confused. He told me he was going to save it for when we came home, and he would open it for Rick and my brothers to share together.

He knew exactly what he was doing. He wanted the reunion, he wanted the family unit to heal, and he wanted me home.

THE TRUMAN SHOW

We were having the time of our lives during those weeks together, and it wasn't because of some grand gesture, or any superficial or material possessions. It was because we were together doing all the things that we had always loved. The simple things. We would walk, go for lunch to my favourite places; we spent time in nature; we sat around a campfire under the stars, talking late into the night; we watched our favourite movies, reciting the scripts and laughing until we

119

cried. We talked about everything and anything. The hours seemed to last only minutes. We were in 'the zone', becoming separated from what we both referred to as the 'Truman Show' going on around us. For the first time in my life, I felt like these moments we were experiencing together were real life and everything else was fake. Questions continued to pop into my mind about this so-called 'normal' life; was it in fact just an illusion? Perhaps we were all being lied to. Perhaps we had been indoctrinated into a society and a culture that was fast asleep. Had I been asleep all this time?

In this sudden state of awareness, and with Syd's terminal diagnosis hanging over our heads, I found the confidence to share with Syd my experience in 2011 watching the documentary *I Am* and how it had changed the way I saw things. To my surprise, he shared with me a similar experience he'd had after watching a film called *The Shift* by Dr Wayne Dyer, a man I had never heard of until that day. It was as if we had given each other permission to share whatever we feared others would label as 'weird'. We didn't know it then, but what we were doing was creating a safe space where there was no judgement and we could be completely vulnerable. Our conversations opened up like a blossoming flower, and our hunger to know more about the meaning of life deepened. There was something happening which I still find difficult to describe in words. It was an awareness of something bigger than both of us. Some people call it God; others call it the universe, spirit, or a higher power. It doesn't matter; it doesn't need a label. It's a *knowing*.

We began to laugh at our own lives and those of others – the so-called first-world problems we all claimed to have suddenly seemed ridiculous. We started to wonder: why were we all so neurotic? Why were so many of us depressed? Why did we experience so much suffering? Why do we lie to ourselves? Despite the dire circumstances we found ourselves in, we both felt a strange sense of excitement and hope, like we had been lost at sea and a rescue boat had appeared on the horizon.

I'M NOT LEAVING!

'Come on, let's go gold class!' I said excitedly.

Syd looked puzzled. 'Why? What's that?'

'Oh my God, it's so good! It's just like business class but in the cinema – it's awesome. Come on, let's do it!' I replied.

I had wanted to take him from the moment he arrived. A new film had been released on 23rd January, and it had our names written all over it. *The Wolf of Wall Street*, starring Leonardo DiCaprio, is the true story of a Wall Street stockbroker, Jordan Belfort – a man whose greed, addictions and life of debauchery caused his life to come crashing down and eventually landed him in prison. We were sold. The fast cars, superyachts, and insight into the mind of a man who took his life to the edge appealed to every part of our being. So we took the one-hour drive to the nearest Westfield shopping centre, took the escalator to the third floor, and entered the gold-class foyer, our eyes wide as saucers. We took our seats on a plush sofa near the bar outside the main screen and started to thumb our way through the menu. We were like a couple of kids in a sweet shop. We marvelled at the fact that we could pre-order our food and have it delivered to our seats at different intervals throughout the show.

'What do you fancy?' I asked, not wanting to be the first to order my body weight in sugar.

'Oooh, let's get waffles, and a sundae, and scones with jam and cream, and maybe a cup of tea?' he said.

'You stick with the tea, mate. I'm having a Prosecco!' I shot back.

'Of course you are,' he laughed, with an eye roll.

We both had a sugar addiction – never went for the savoury, always the sweet. And I most definitely had an unfavourable alcohol dependency. Happy and content with our dopamine-triggering choices and thirty-minute delivery intervals, we sank down into our huge red velour reclining seats in front of the ginormous screen. In that moment I remember feeling so incredibly happy. It wouldn't seem like anything special to anyone else, but as we sat in those chairs, we shared an incredible closeness that I hadn't felt for years. We were in heaven, our own little piece of heaven.

We raved about the film all the way home, laughing uncontrollably and impersonating the characters from our favourite scenes, but then as we re-enacted one particular scene, I was stopped in my tracks. As the FBI are closing in on Jordan and his criminal activity, he knows his time is up and he can't escape the inevitable. He's advised by both his father and his lawyer to resign from his company and save himself, but right at the last minute he does a complete U-turn and decides to stay. In front of all his staff, he shouts down the microphone, like a man possessed, 'I'm not leaving! I'm not leaving!' As I glanced across at Syd from the passenger seat and watched as he recreated the scene, all I could think about was his cancer – it was closing in on him and he couldn't escape. All I wanted him to do was to start screaming, 'I'm not leaving! I'm not leaving!' Selfishly, I needed him to tell me he wasn't going to leave me.

That night, my grief made itself known for the first time. It had been hiding out underneath all the smiles and laughter of the prior weeks. Then, as if out of nowhere, the reality of what we were facing finally hit me. I was blindsided, like I had been hit by a ten-ton truck. Although we didn't speak about it in the car, we both sensed the conversation slowing down, and the silence became so loud it was deafening. He knew what I was thinking, and I knew he knew. The minute my head touched the pillow that night, I could sense my body rising and falling; a ball of dark energy gripped my insides, like nothing I had ever felt before. I was out of control. I tried desperately to make it stop, push it down, but as I tried to walk to the bathroom, my legs just wouldn't hold me up. My entire body was shaking, and like a river bursting its banks, the tears began to flow uncontrollably. I fell to my knees and began to release what I can only describe as the wails of a grieving mother who had lost her baby. I couldn't believe this noise was coming out of my own body, and I couldn't make it stop. Without panic, Rick calmly pulled the covers back, stepped out of bed and sat beside me on the floor of our bathroom. He held me tight. He didn't say a word.

In July, six months after Syd left Australia and returned to the UK, he sent me an email. It said:

> *To my big sister, a message just for you. Coming to see you was one of the best things I ever did.*
> *I think about the time I spent with you every day and miss you a huge amount. You mean the world to me, and I am counting down the time until I get back on that plane and that's the truth.*
> *I feel like me and you still have a lot to experience together and that's one of the reasons I won't be leaving this world too early.*

All I heard was 'I'M NOT LEAVING!'

CHAPTER EIGHT:
THE ALTERNATIVE PATH

The cure of many diseases is unknown to
physicians because they are ignorant of the whole.
For the part can never be well unless the
whole is well.
Plato

When I started my career in medical sales, I had a relatively naive attitude towards healthcare and most healthcare professionals. If I ever visited the doctor's surgery – which was thankfully rare – I trusted that the doctor sitting behind the desk with their qualifications littering the walls knew everything they needed to know in order to keep me healthy, and more importantly to keep me well informed on the ways I could keep myself healthy. This largely came from being brought up to respect anyone in authority and never to question their decisions, even if they didn't seem to make sense – because of course they knew better than me. They were 'qualified'. This attitude was encouraged not only by the medical industry but also by the police, the church, and of course my school. All of these people, as I understood it, knew better than me, and I was to listen, learn, and do as I was told. I was suffering from a terrible affliction called 'blind faith'.

Now, I want to say from the outset that I'm not positing

an argument here either for or against the medical industry – and I do have the utmost respect for all my fellow human beings, doctors or not. What I present in this chapter is my own personal experience – my discovery that what I had been taught was wrong.

The healthcare services we have access to, particularly here in the UK, are incredible. If we are acutely unwell as the result of, let's say, a heart attack, a stroke, or some trauma like a road traffic accident, then there is a high chance that we will survive. It's truly remarkable what can be done now to save someone who would have surely died only fifty years ago. We are very good at what I call the 'mechanics of healthcare': putting bodies back together again. The problem is, we are not machines. Take this analogy that I once heard as an example. If you were to take your car apart, cut the doors off, take out the windows, remove the exhaust, the wheels, the chassis, and scatter it all in tiny little pieces across the floor, every nut and bolt, you could then, with the right tools and knowledge, put it all back together and it would work perfectly. Now imagine if you took your dog apart in the same way, cutting it up into tiny little pieces, first the legs, then the ears, then take out the heart, the lungs, the liver etc., and scatter the pieces across the floor, there would be no doubt in your mind that you would not be able to put it back together again – right? That's because we are innately different to machines. We are not just a mechanical body. We have a mind, a body, and a spirit. There is a life force running through us. We are a huge ball of whirling cells, nerves, chemicals, energy, and tissue, some of which you can see and some of which you cannot. And if you want to go one step further and examine yourself at the quantum level, you will discover that you are in fact made up of 99.9 per cent space. That's right – we are nothingness. And to make things even more complicated, we are all completely unique – all eight billion of us.

Healing the human body requires much more than just mechanics. It requires integrated, holistic healthcare with the patient at its centre, not the symptom-focused healthcare we have now whereby we treat the manifestations of disease rather than focusing on the root cause. The key word here is 'integrated'. What we currently have is what many refer to as the band-aid solution, meaning there is only one way in which chronic diseases are treated: using pharmaceutical drugs to control symptoms of an underlying and often bigger problem. Essentially, we are plugging the holes that have appeared in the pipes instead of turning the water off at the tap– or, as Desmond Tutu once said, 'We need to stop pulling people out of the river. We need to go upstream and find out why they're falling in.'

Here are some examples of how the band-aid solution works. We go to the doctor; we are told we have diabetes, but rather than being educated about good nutrition– avoiding highly processed foods and sugar, reducing the amount we eat and increasing our intake of organic whole foods– we are all too often only handed a prescription for a blood-sugar-lowering medication and sent on our way. Or let's say we go to the doctor with symptoms of anxiety and depression.

Rather than benefiting from a disease-centred approach, focusing on the trauma or related incident (the 'why') that perhaps caused the depression in the first place, we are instead given an antidepressant drug and reviewed after six months – if we're lucky. At worst, we're completely lost in the system and left with a repeat prescription for the next thirty years . . . or, even worse, we suffer further health issues: drug or alcohol dependency, and in the worst cases death by suicide or substance abuse.

And then, of course, there's cancer. A cancer diagnosis is typically followed by the offer of three treatment pathways (the only options available to us): surgery, chemotherapy, and radiation – also known as cut, poison, and burn. And while some of these treatments may be effective to a degree, we can't ignore the statistics. According to Cancer Research UK, one in two of us will be diagnosed with cancer in our lifetime, and approximately fifty per cent of us will not survive. That leaves approximately fifty per cent of us who will survive, right? Wrong. In 2017 I attended an oncology nursing conference in Adelaide, where I listened to numerous oncologists speak. I took notes – including this, taken straight from the horse's mouth: 'There is no cure for cancer using the treatments we are currently using. The best we can achieve is to maintain or stabilise the disease.'

So, although it appears we are making progress on survival, that only relates to survival within a five-year window. This is stabilisation of the disease. The survival rate beyond five years has not improved. Unfortunately, the statistics presented to us regarding cancer survival rates are typically based on five-year survival only, so they are not a true representation of what's actually happening. Regardless, one thing is painfully clear: what we are doing isn't working. According to Worldometer which measures a number of global statistics in 'real time', currently approximately eight million people die every year globally from cancer-related diseases. Since President Nixon announced the beginning of the so-called 'war on cancer' in the early seventies, the progress to find a cure for cancers has remained largely stagnant for over forty years. That's despite the billions of pounds that have been funnelled into cancer research and what seems like the never-ending, heartbreaking fundraisers run by cancer patients and their families and friends – me included – every year. We may know more about cancer than we did forty years ago, but we're no closer to a cure. Why not? Could it be possible that we have been looking in the wrong places all along? I strongly believe so.

THE WHOLE

Let me be clear: I'm not saying that all conventional treatments are bad and don't work – but what I am saying is that they come at a price, they often don't address the root cause, and they are most certainly not a magic bullet. So, why isn't there a different approach to mainstream medicine? I don't believe there is one definitive answer to this question, but let me share a few things I've learnt during my time in the healthcare industry that might help shine a light on the problem.

When I became a sales representative for one of the largest medical device companies in the world, I felt so lucky, like all my Christmases had come at once. However, despite my enthusiasm and excitement in the early days of my career, I suffered from a bad case of imposter syndrome. The vast majority of the national team of sales representatives (of whom there were about 150) were fully fledged healthcare professionals – and if they weren't healthcare professionals, they at least had a university degree. I wasn't one and didn't have the other. I felt 'less than' from the very outset. But I drew on what my dad refers to as my 'challenger of life' attitude and focused on how I could use the skills I did have to learn the ropes as quickly as possible. I had a desire to be the best I could be, so I set about absorbing as much information as I could from the people I worked with most closely.

I can remember one of my first road trips with a colleague down to a remote part of South Australia. She was an intensive care nurse by trade but had worked in the world of medical sales for many years. She was a warm and friendly woman, and we hit it off straight away. She was about fifteen years older than me and lived in the beautiful Adelaide Hills region. We shared a love of all things English, in particular the glorious countryside. She was someone I felt drawn to straight away, not only because of her bubbly character and her tremendous amount of knowledge but because I felt like she was taking me under her wing – I felt safe with her. As I sat in the passenger seat of her white Subaru, feeling slightly nervous and awkward, I plucked up the courage to ask her if she would teach me everything she knew about wound care (this would be my specialty). She didn't hesitate, and proceeded to download her brain onto me there and then. As we hurtled down the freeway, I scribbled notes as fast as I could, trying to keep up. I asked her to repeat anything I didn't understand until I finally felt like I had mastered it. She was so animated and passionate about everything she said, and I can remember thinking 'I want to be just like her'.

It didn't take me long to pick things up. I had found my 'sweet spot' – a career I felt I could garner true meaning and purpose in. A couple of months later, I attended my first national sales conference in Sydney. At that conference, I got my first glimpse of the reasons for our band-aid society. As part of my training, it was imperative that I understood the anatomy and physiology of the human body, and the holistic management of wound healing. As I listened intently during education sessions, I picked up on a wonderful phrase – it was a phrase I would use at every teaching session I facilitated later, and it would stay with me throughout my eight years in medical sales and beyond: 'When it comes to healing wounds, it's not just about the hole in the person, it's about the whole of the person.'

It was so simple. It made total sense to me. Why would we try to fix the physical wound in the body if we didn't address the underlying causes? The wound would surely never heal. So surely the same logic and approach should be applied to treating all chronic diseases? I started to question why it was necessary for a seemingly less educated individual like me to be educating and training degree-qualified doctors and nurses on this very subject. Didn't they receive training on wound management? I was shocked to discover that the answer was: no, not really. It's widely understood in the medical industry, but was unknown to me at the time, that physicians receive approximately eight hours of wound care education during their five years of training. Worse still, they receive only ten to twenty-four hours of nutritional education. Their core competencies throughout their training tend to focus around physical examinations, diagnostics, documentation, prescribing pharmaceutical drugs, and symptom management – the 'mechanics'.

I quickly became aware that there was a problem at the grassroots level. We were ignoring the whole person.

MONEY, MONEY, MONEY

None of this would be an issue, of course, if the system were working. But it is agonisingly clear that it's not. According to the Office of National Statistics, our expenditure on healthcare in the UK alone was £225 billion in 2019. This was before the COVID-19 pandemic in 2020, when it jumped up twenty per cent to £269 billion. When you compare this to the £140.8 billion spent in 2010, you can see this is an astronomical increase, and not reflective of a healthy society. Not only that, according to the NHS BSA Website; we are spending £17.2 billion on pharmaceutical drugs each year – yet people are getting sicker, not better. It's often said that the definition of insanity is doing the same thing over and over again and expecting different results. What we have is an insane healthcare system. What we need is an integrated, holistic healthcare system that is not only governed and regulated responsibly but made available and accessible to all.

TAKING CONTROL

After a few months of thrashing around in rough seas, surrounded by anger, grief, and disillusionment following Syd's terminal diagnosis, I decided to get out of the water, dry myself off, and put my big-girl pants on. I was acutely aware that there was so much I couldn't control, so the only thing left to do was to start focusing on the things that I could. Being out of control isn't something most people are comfortable with – and I come from a long family lineage of control freaks, so for me it was incredibly unsettling. I wasn't willing to accept Syd's terminal diagnosis, and luckily neither was he. I still had so many questions, and had a feeling there were more options out there for him than we were being told about. The first step in finding some answers to those questions came by chance when I attended a customer meeting at a small suburban hospital in South Australia.

I was visiting one of the clinical managers there – I'll call him Barry – to discuss his wound care education needs for the department. This was a pretty routine meeting. But as we sat and talked, our conversation quickly turned to my brother's diagnosis. As I sat there in his office explaining all about Syd's rare cancer and my despair that no one knew anything about it, I could sense my emotions bubbling to the surface.

Barry could see I was struggling. He tipped his head to one side in sympathy and said, 'Well, maybe I can help, even if it's only a little. You may not know, but my wife is an oncology nurse here at the hospital, and I think she may be able to help you, or at least put you in touch with some people who can.'

It turned out that the hospital I was sitting in was the only hospital in South Australia that treated patients for neuroendocrine cancer. What were the chances?! Barry told me that they were connected to a charity-based organisation called the Unicorn Foundation which had patient support group meetings every month in the city. He suggested that I look them up and perhaps they would have some answers to my questions. I thanked him and left his office.

As soon as I returned home, I got the laptop out and started to research everything I could about the organisation and its mission. Not long after that, I plucked up the courage to attend one of the patient support group meetings. Imposter syndrome descended on me like a black cloud once again. What would everyone think of me turning up at a meeting where everyone had been diagnosed with cancer except me? I felt somehow embarrassed, as if I wasn't worthy of being in the same room as people going through the most challenging health issue of their lives. I felt like I would just be in the way and waste everyone's time; strange how the mind plays such tricks on us. My thoughts were running rampant.

I gave myself a good talking-to and finally accepted that what I was thinking was ridiculous. I reminded myself that I had one mission: to save Syd's life. I was there to gather as much information as I could for Syd, to give him the best chance of survival. Who could refuse that?

So, one sunny Tuesday afternoon in the autumn of 2014, I walked into my first patient support group meeting. It was held at the Cancer Council building, which was located right on the southern fringe of Adelaide's central business district. As I popped my head around the door, I could see people sitting on a circle of chairs in the centre of the room.

'Hello, is this the Unicorn Foundation meeting?' I said nervously.

I was immediately met with the warmest of welcomes. As I took my seat, I put my bag on the floor and plucked out my notebook. Before I had chance to write a word, I was kindly ushered across the room to where the tea- and coffee-making facilities were; cradling my cup of hot tea in my hands, I walked back to my seat and settled in to listen and soak up all the information I could. One thing I noticed immediately was that not one person looked sick – not one. How could they all have cancer when they all looked so well? We are often bombarded with images of cancer patients with bald heads, pale skin, and skinny frames, but the reality is quite different, especially for patients suffering with neuroendocrine cancer. I also noticed the varying age groups; some people were my age, and others were in their fifties and sixties.

The room fell silent before one of the patients announced a quick icebreaker. I started to sink into my seat. I felt a shot of anxiety leap through my body as I suddenly became aware I was going to have to introduce myself and explain my story. As each person introduced themselves and told the story of their cancer diagnosis, I could feel a sense of panic. I was trying my best to listen, but all I could think of was what I was going to say. *I am a fake, a phony. I don't have cancer. I don't know why I am here.* I was fast regretting my presence and felt the urge to run for the door. But before I could, it was my turn.

I had a few minutes to tell my story, and to my surprise it was met with the most wonderful kindness, compassion and understanding. Not only that, but everyone was so interested to hear about Syd's cancer and our unique story of battling the disease from one side of the world to the other. I suddenly had a bunch of people I could relate to, and they could relate to me. My imposter syndrome was well and truly extinguished when I realised that three patients were in attendance with a sibling or spouse. One of the patients' sisters introduced herself and explained she was there to be an advocate for her sister. She wanted to understand everything about her disease and explore every possible avenue with regard to available and effective treatments. She wanted to know how she could help in what felt like a helpless situation. Their story reflected ours, and that felt so comforting. I suddenly felt safe and accepted, and I knew I had found my tribe.

I attended these patient support meetings for the next three years. They were the reason I built the confidence to be able to pick up the phone and find the best care possible for Syd in the UK. These meetings gave me access to the leading oncologists and nuclear medicine specialists in Australia. Without their support, I would have found it almost impossible to make sense of Syd's scans; the terminology was mind-boggling at times. I was finally able to get my questions answered.

I wanted to do anything I could to help the cause, too, so I set up a little fundraising page on Facebook called 'Love Your Brother'. I wanted to raise awareness and spread the word that more needed to be done to help people suffering with rare cancers. They didn't get any airtime, so I wanted to create some for them. I got involved in organising fundraising events, raising over $70,000. Both Rick and the boys got involved with me, supporting me every step of the way. It was the outlet I needed, and the support I was receiving from the friendships I'd built with these amazing people kept me more motivated than I had ever been. I had found hope. I had found light in my darkness. And the best thing about it all was: I had given hope to Syd. As long as he was breathing, I was going to stop at nothing to get him as many answers as I could.

THE TRUTH ABOUT CANCER

Despite Syd being offered a couple of chemotherapy-based treatments, the story remained the same: any evidence to support the effectiveness of these treatments was limited, and therefore he remained steadfast in resisting them. He couldn't see any logic in harming his body with only a ten per cent chance of it having any effect on the cancer. He would laugh when he told me how his doctor explained that one of the side effects of the proposed chemotherapy was that he would likely develop secondary cancer within ten years: a treatment for cancer which causes cancer. He kept repeating, 'It just doesn't make any sense.' What we needed to do was to explore other avenues. But what were those avenues? We didn't really know. We had some knowledge of alternative treatments, but it was fairly limited, so we knew we needed to up the ante.

Naturally curious and extremely stubborn as I am, it was clear I would stop at nothing until I had all the information I needed. I started to read anything I could get my hands on that would demonstrate remarkable healing in other people who had supposedly lost all hope – people who were diagnosed as terminally ill and somehow survived, despite all the odds being against them. I found myself drawn to books about the mind–body connection, the power of our immune system, and our incredible ability as humans to heal ourselves. I literally became obsessed, inhaling any literature I could get my hands on. Syd would joke I was like Johnny 5, the famous robot from the film *Short Circuit*, gasping 'need more input'. I was so thirsty for knowledge.

Then one day in October 2015 I scrolled through my Facebook news feed and stumbled across a documentary series called *The Truth about Cancer*. This would be a game changer. I watched the brief trailer which outlined what the series was all about, and I intuitively knew I had to watch it – I could hear my inner voice loud and clear. The series was due to start that very month, with a new episode airing every day for nine days. I called Syd and told him that we needed to watch the episodes in real time, from one side of the world to the other, and make the commitment to take notes and report back with our learnings.

Sitting on my bed with a notebook and pen, I watched and listened in shock as I was taken through the first episode. I was dumbfounded. How was it that during all of my school years I couldn't remember a time when I had been taught any of the information I was now being given? Important historical information about the formation of the medical system as we know it; the corruption, lies, and control; the censorship of natural (so-called 'alternative') therapies; and the countless case studies and testimonials of people who had healed themselves using these very therapies. Why was all this information hidden from the mainstream? Why were so many natural therapies being censored? Slowly but surely, I could see a pattern emerging, and I discovered that to find the answers to my questions, all I had to do was follow the money.

When Syd was diagnosed with cancer and eventually given a terminal diagnosis, we were only told half a story. Was this because the doctors didn't care about him? Of course not; just like the majority of human beings, they were trying to do their best with what they knew. But just like any parent who is trying to do their best when raising their children, they can't help the fact that they don't know what they don't know. They don't have all the information available to them. The problem is the system they operate in. I've already mentioned that doctors receive little or no training in nutrition and wound care, but alternative therapies and holistic, integrative pathways are also missing from their curriculum. Many other healing modalities are available around the world – it's just that they don't fit into the mainstream model of care.

When it comes to our health, surely having all of the information available to us so that we can make informed decisions is the best way forward? Wouldn't you want to know everything? That is why it's so important that if something doesn't feel right, you must keep asking questions. If you're still not satisfied, do your own research. If you need a second opinion, or a third, or fourth, don't be afraid to ask for it. If you are the person suffering from a terminal illness, find someone you can trust to be your advocate, someone to be your voice, someone who will fight for you when you are too exhausted to fight. Do not fall into the trap of blind faith. You have the power to direct your own healing. It will empower you; it will give you hope and a sense of control in what can be a desperately out-of-control situation.

By the time we reached the end of all nine episodes, I was utterly exhausted. My brain felt like it had a million filing cabinets open with paper spewing out everywhere. I didn't know where to start, or how to put everything away neatly.

I remembered more wise words from Desmond Tutu: 'There is only one way to eat an elephant: a bite at a time'. So we started small. Using the knowledge we had, we could take one element at a time and put it into practice. And we had a guide – seven essential elements to adopt which would allow Syd to take control of his own cancer diagnosis. You will notice I have highlighted some in bold. These are the elements that my inner voice was telling me were going to be critical in Syd's own path towards healing:

1. Letting food be your medicine
2. Detoxing
3. **Balancing your energy**
4. **Healing your emotional wounds**
5. Biological dentistry
6. Using specific herbs and vitamins
7. True prevention

As my obsessive research continued, I would come across a similar list, this time taken from a book called *Radical Remission* by Kelly A. Turner, PhD. This book details the personal stories of patients who recovered from cancer against all the odds; these are the nine factors that directly influenced their healing:

1. Changing your diet
2. Taking control of your health
3. Following your intuition
4. Using herbs and supplements
5. **Releasing suppressed emotions**
6. Increasing positive emotions

7. Embracing social support
8. **Deepening your spiritual connection**
9. **Having strong reasons for living**

I was beginning to notice patterns appearing and what seemed like signposts guiding us towards perhaps some sort of healing, I started to believe a miracle could happen.

CHAPTER NINE: A WEEKEND IN MELBOURNE

If you change the way you look at things,
the things you look at change.
Wayne Dyer

It was 2015, and my determination to be the 'fixer' was in full swing. I wasn't only trying my hardest to heal Syd; I was also in the throes of trying to heal my husband and our marriage. Despite months of calm and some of the happiest moments of my life throughout our time together, there were also months of chaos and sadness. Rick's depression hit an all-time low. His symptoms were uncontrolled and poorly managed, and this was often the catalyst for the storm that ensued. He repeatedly attended doctors' appointments but would only ever be given a repeat prescription for antidepressants and Valium, or told to increase the dosage – with zero follow-up. He would come home from these appointments deflated and at a loss. He didn't feel listened to or cared for in the way that he so desperately needed and hoped for. However, there was one doctor – our family GP in the early days of living in Australia – who gave him hope of getting better.

Dr S was one of those doctors who was always booked up for weeks and forever ran over on his appointments. He showed deep compassion and empathy towards Rick's situation and would often give him hope when he couldn't see light at the end of the tunnel. He was so different to every other doctor Rick had ever seen, a real breath of fresh air. For once, Rick felt he might get the help he needed.

One day, after seeing Dr S routinely for over a year, Rick called to make an appointment with him. There was a pause at the end of the line. As the receptionist began to speak, Rick knew by the tone of her voice that something was wrong.

'I'm so sorry, but Dr S passed away last week,' she said hesitantly.

Rick paused, then said, 'I just can't believe it – what happened?'

She proceeded to explain that Dr S had taken his own life. We were both in shock. Neither of us saw that coming. But suddenly it became clear to both of us why he understood Rick's depression and his need to be heard, and why he was so empathetic. It was another reminder to us all that we never know what someone is going through, and we must always be kind.

Following Dr S's tragic death, the revolving door of doctors began again. Rick was so frustrated. He didn't want to be on medication for the rest of his life – I am yet to meet anyone who does – and yet medication seemed to be all that was on offer. He was losing trust in the system. On one occasion, he was referred to a clinical psychiatrist, and after a one-hour appointment focusing purely on his symptoms, he was sent home with a prescription for double the dose of his antidepressants and a strong antiseizure medication with some worrying side effects, including– wait for it– an increased risk of suicide. Rick couldn't believe it. He threw the prescription away and sat on the sofa with his head in his hands. He was so discouraged. He didn't know which way to turn, and I was worried he was beaten. But somehow, he would find the strength to pull himself back together and carry on.

For me, living with his depression felt like I was living inside a pinball machine, getting shot in different directions each day, not knowing whether I would hit the target or roll down into the hole at the bottom. I felt at the mercy of his ever-changing highs and lows, which would feel like a constant sledgehammer to my highly sensitive being. But despite the painful roundabout we seemed to be stuck on, I had a deep knowing that this was all part of the process – it was essential to our growth together as a couple and, more importantly, as individuals.

I would literally do anything I could to try to help the situation. I would leave books on the side, open on specific pages that would describe how I was feeling, hoping he would read them. I would push for him to see counsellors and therapists, hoping he would go, but he didn't; like so many people suffering with depression, he'd lost faith after many failed attempts at finding the right therapist. I considered writing an email to every member of his family to tell them exactly what was happening and all of my worries – an intervention of sorts, maybe a cry for help– but I was too fearful of what his reaction might be and I wanted to protect his privacy. In the back of my mind, I think I was worried it would look like

I'd failed if I asked for help; I would often think to myself that I should be able to manage on my own. I was also facing the fact that he didn't seem to want help, despite how desperate he seemed at times. He was often in self-sabotage mode, which is extremely common for those suffering with depression. I would see him as two different people: his false self and his true self – just as I saw mirrored in myself. When he acted out of fear, expressing anger, jealousy, guilt, and shame, in my head I would categorise this as his false self. When he acted out of love, expressing affection, kindness, compassion, vulnerability, gentleness, and intimacy – I would categorise this as his true self. Compartmentalising everything that was going on helped me to make sense of the situation.

His struggles often acted as a mirror reflecting back my own struggles. He was just another human being exhausted by his own suffering. He wasn't angry with me; he was angry with himself. I didn't need to take this personally, though that was easier said than done. But my perspective was changing – I was coming at it from a different angle, and that gave me a small sense of liberation. None of this was my fault, nor was it his; it was just a life situation we had found ourselves in, and the blame needed to be removed. What I knew for sure was that no matter how difficult things became, one thing remained true for both of us: our deep love for one another. And it was that true, unquestionable love that would winch us out of the stormy waters, rescue us and put us gently back onto dry land time and again.

YES MAN

Something had shifted in me following Syd's visit in 2014. I was starting to open up more and be less fearful. I was interested in exploring the subject of spirituality – something I had avoided for years due to my early exposure to Christianity and Catholicism, which had left me feeling confused and misaligned.

As a child, religion frightened me. This is how I saw it: if you're good, you go to heaven, and if you're bad, you go to hell. So, naturally, I wanted to be a good girl. And if I was ever bad, I just wouldn't tell anyone. For many people, religion can be the birthplace of shame.

I can remember finding all the religious rituals, the pomp and the ceremony a little strange and intimidating. One memory in particular still sticks in my mind. When I was around seven years old, I would attend our local Baptist church with my mum on Sundays. I would watch on as grown men and women were baptised in a giant indoor pool. I cannot explain why, but this really scared me. I think it was perhaps the fact that it appeared to be some sort of mass drowning. The chosen members of the congregation would approach the pool in a line; each one would step into the water, fully clothed, and the priest would drop them backward and fully immerse them in the pool. I'm sure they weren't gasping for air as they came up, but as an impressionable child I would soak up this ritual, thinking they were all crazy – and drowning. I couldn't understand what on earth was going on. It was a child's interpretation, but a traumatic one nonetheless.

Even though there seemed to be a lot of messages of love, joy, and hope in church, unfortunately they often seemed to get lost in messages of condemnation, original sin, and the threat of hell. It all seemed very conflicting to me. What I did love about church, however, was the joy of singing, reading and dancing; the general feeling of togetherness and connection with the community; and how kind, generous, happy, and friendly everyone in the congregation seemed to be – well, for that one day of the week, at least. Most human beings didn't seem to be able to make that stick beyond Sundays. Christmas was the same. What my little brain really couldn't process, though, was the idea of a man up in the sky calling all the shots. It didn't seem plausible at all. I was calling bullshit.

On reflection, I can see it was the religious dogmatism that kept me cut off and starved from my spirit, my soul – my true source. The truth I came to know for myself was that God wasn't a man in the sky with a long beard, sitting on a golden throne, wearing flowing white robes; God was an energy, a life force running through me that was connected to every living thing in the universe. Syd's diagnosis was what brought me back to that 'source' energy. I was reunited with my faith. It was around this time that I started saying yes to life. I stopped holding back. I wanted to experience more of life and follow what felt right. What would happen if I said yes to everything – ignored the fear and just jumped in – stopped making excuses and let life flow through me?

One day, I got the opportunity to test the strategy out.

I was lying in bed one Saturday morning, sometime around April 2015. The sun was shining, and I was in my happy place, warm and cosy, snuggled up in bed with my head buried in Rick's arms. It was that glorious moment on a Saturday morning when you have nowhere to be and nothing to do. Rick had already been up to get breakfast started and I could hear the kettle boiling, and the smell of bacon cooking drifted into the room, making my tummy rumble. I glanced out of the window and picked up my phone to start my morning ritual of scrolling through social media. Up popped an advert for an event hosted by none other than Dr Wayne Dyer, and my interest was immediately sparked. The event was titled 'I Am Light' and was to be held in Melbourne for a full weekend in August. Every cell of my being screamed 'Yes!' It seemed like a sign – I had been studying Wayne's teachings, he was someone Syd and I shared a passion for, and the event had the words 'I Am' in the title. How could I not go? But immediately the excuses crept in. *It's too far, I don't have the time, I can't afford it, I can't go on my own* . . . it went on. In that moment, as I tried to bat away the excuses swarming like bees around my head, I turned to Rick and said, 'Look, I know this is going to sound really weird to you, but there's this event in Melbourne in August with Wayne Dyer and I really want to go. It's an entire weekend, so it will mean paying for not just the tickets, but a hotel room and the flights – what do you think?'

Without a moment of hesitation, he said 'Just go. If you want to go, then just do it. It doesn't matter about the money or how far away it is. Just go!'

I was seeking permission outside of myself. Why do we often think it's more important to seek permission from others than to give permission to ourselves? It didn't matter why; it worked. I quickly tapped on the 'buy now' button and purchased my ticket. Within half an hour, I had my hotel room and my flights booked. I just knew something magical was going to happen.

IT'S UP TO YOU

As I closed the front door, I was torn. Should I stay, or should I go? I had been in this position before, many times. But until this day, I had always given in and put Rick's feelings before my own. I would back down and say sorry and just try to kiss it all better. But on this day, I felt an urge to be firm and exercise some boundaries. The memory is so vivid because it was the very first time this had happened to me. I felt like a mother having to give out tough love. His depression was out of control and only made worse by the fact that his way of dealing with it was to get out of his mind – literally. It wasn't the answer to his problems, but I have learnt over time that when you're suffering from mental and emotional pain, it can often seem like the only way to survive in that moment. He was attempting to escape his own mind using substances, but the problem was that his pain and suffering would only return with a vengeance the next day, and the day after that.

The timing couldn't have been worse. I was leaving for my trip to Melbourne, and I was faced with having to overcome my feelings of guilt at leaving him alone for the weekend. At the same time, I was angry that he was doing this to me – to us. There had to be consequences to his behaviour; I couldn't keep 'fixing things' for him. This was about my own self-preservation; I had to put myself first, and remain steadfast and strong. With tears streaming down my face, I turned my keys in the ignition and pulled out of the driveway. I kept my eyes on the road and my mind on the weekend ahead. I didn't look back.

I arrived at the Melbourne Convention Centre in what I would now call a surrendered state. I had no answers any more; I was ready to give in and let something bigger than me take over. I felt utterly drained. I was alone and a little scared, but surprisingly comforted by being away in another part of the country – away from the chaos, surrounded by like-minded people. I didn't know what to expect. I had never attended anything like this before.

As I walked into the main foyer, I was handed a goodie bag at the reception desk and directed into the main lecture theatre. I was overwhelmed when I realised there were one thousand people in attendance in just one room. I chose a seat at random, in the middle, to the right of the centre stage.

Like an excited first-year student, I took out my notebook and a pen and waited patiently for it all to begin. There was a palpable sense of anticipation in the air. I think when you're in a room with so many other humans, it's impossible not to feel the energy. It felt wonderful. In his book *Awe*, Dacher Keltner refers to this as 'collective effervescence'.

As I waited for the event to start, I couldn't help but hear two young women in front of me talking about their flight over; it turned out they had also travelled from Adelaide. Everybody in that room had travelled from all over the world, yet by some chance I had chosen to sit right behind two people from Adelaide – coincidence? They seemed so excited, throwing their heads back in laughter as they continued chatting away. I couldn't help but feel pangs of jealousy; in that moment, I felt so alone. I took a breath, swallowed my nerves, and introduced myself. I quickly discovered that not only were they from Adelaide, but we also shared a mutual friend – how could this be? It was the very same friend I had met at the airport in 2010. This wasn't a coincidence, this was synchronicity. It felt like they were placed right in my path on purpose, and they were. They saved me that weekend – it was a case of 'women supporting women' at its best. We spent the evening together at a local restaurant, and we listened to each other's stories late into the evening. I no longer felt alone.

Just before Wayne entered the room, the excitement was peaking. As I sat waiting patiently, I began rustling through my goodie bag. In it there were pens, a notebook, a couple of gifted books . . . and then I noticed two randomly selected cards. They were oracle cards. You know the type – the ones with celestial images on them, with a supporting affirmation. As I lifted mine out of the bag, I couldn't quite believe it when I held them out in front of me. They read 'Let Go' and 'It's Up To You'.

It was another lightbulb moment. I had a sudden realisation that I was the reason for my own suffering. I was my own problem. Not Rick, not my family, not anyone. I had become the sum of all the choices I'd made. I had been telling myself a story about myself. A victim story. In that moment, I knew it was time to change my thoughts. It was going to change my life.

SOUL SHIFT

It's difficult to put into words the change in me that occurred after that weekend, but what stuck with me the most was the concept that I was in fact a spiritual being having a human experience, not the other way around. Everything I had ever thought about life seemed to have been flipped on its head. So many profound truths and pieces of wisdom came through Wayne that weekend, and I just couldn't get enough. I knew this had changed the direction of my life. It was as if a whole new world had been opened up to me. But, strangely, this wasn't an unrecognisable world; it was somehow a world I had once known but had completely forgotten about. It felt so familiar, like an old memory had resurfaced. I had a deep realisation that I wasn't just the wife, the mother, the sister, the daughter, the employee, or the friend – these were just parts I was playing. I once heard Eckhart Tolle call this our 'personal reality', or personality. I wasn't any of those things. At the core of my being, I was light – nothing more and nothing less. I knew I needed to connect with that part of myself. That was where my power was.

Just seven days later, I would find myself sitting in Adelaide Airport, on my way to Darwin. I was flicking through my news feed, waiting for my flight to start boarding, when suddenly it popped up on my screen: Dr Wayne Dyer had gone to sleep and never woke up.

Once I got past the initial shock, I pondered on how special and perfectly synchronistic it was to have been in his presence during what would be his final spiritual masterclass.

CHAPTER TEN:
MIRACLES HAPPEN

Miracles reawaken the awareness that the spirit,
not the body, is the altar of truth.
This is the recognition that leads to the
healing power of the miracle.
A Course in Miracles

On 15th September 2016, I wrote in my journal: 'Syd's scan results came back showing no progression or new tumours, some stable and three have shrunk slightly'.

A miracle had occurred.

CANAL WALKS

Rewind to nine months earlier. I had fully immersed myself in all things natural and alternative. I couldn't unlearn everything I had learnt over the past six months, and I figured that even if I didn't have cancer, I needed to do everything I could to prevent a future diagnosis – plus, it gave me the opportunity to show my love and support for my brother and would hopefully encourage him to take the steps he needed to give himself the best possible chance of survival.

We both got into juicing, eating more organic whole-foods and less garbage, taking supplements, doing regular exercise and using essential oils, and generally became more conscious and aware of what we were putting into our bodies. But there was something niggling inside of me that what I really needed to focus on was my stress and repressed emotions. Through all my research, I started to unearth mounting evidence to support the fact that repressed emotions seemed to be the cause of much of our stress, leading to chronic 'disease' in our society.

I started to look for ways I could begin to uncover and release my own emotions; I had a gut feeling that they were blocking up my insides. It was around this time that I discovered the healing practice of reiki. I have to admit I was a little sceptical at first, but after a little bit of reading I took the plunge and made my first appointment, in a suburb close to the city. As with any therapy, reiki is often only as good as the person delivering it, so I felt lucky that I managed to find someone I clicked with instantly. If you're not familiar with reiki, it's an energetic therapy whereby a practitioner lays their hands on areas of your body and uses the universal energy (also referred to as *chi* or *prana*, meaning 'vital life force') that we all possess to transfer and aid the release of energetic blockages throughout the body and mind. Some people describe being able to feel this energy moving throughout their body as they receive therapy and are often able to achieve a deep meditative state in which they can experience a number of visualisations – and I was no exception. Let me share this example with you.

In 2015 I lost a friend to cancer; ironically, she had the same cancer as my brother. She was initially diagnosed with lung cancer, and later received a second diagnosis of neuroendocrine cancer. It was such a shock. She was only in her thirties, and had never smoked. Her symptoms began with a cough that wouldn't clear up and became so painful and unbearable that she took herself to the emergency department at the local hospital. Following a number of scans and a misdiagnosis of flu and a chest infection, where she was sent home, an MRI scan finally revealed the cancer hiding in her lungs. Out of the blue, she contacted me via social media; we hadn't seen each other for over four years. She had been following our story and wanted to catch up and find out more about neuroendocrine cancer. So, without hesitation, we tied up a lunch date at a local café. We talked and talked for what seemed like hours. We talked about Syd's cancer, her cancer, the desperation of both, and the strange joy of experiencing unconditional love following a terminal diagnosis. As our lunch came to an end, we both rose from our seats and hugged goodbye, and just as she turned to leave, she said, 'Hey, Kay, don't forget – miracles do happen.'

For some reason, what she said that day lit me up inside. It gave me hope. I would repeat her words over and over in my mind for the weeks and months following our meet-up. It became my internal mantra. *Miracles happen.*

A few months later, after one of my monthly reiki sessions, I sat opposite my therapist and she said to me, as she often did, 'How did that feel for you?'

To which I replied, 'Well, I could feel the warmth coming from your hands and I could feel the energy literally moving through my body, it was amazing.'

'Yes, I felt it too – there was a lot of powerful energy there today. Do you mind if I tell you something that came up?'

'Of course!' I said excitedly, eager to hear what she had to say.

'Do the words "miracles happen" mean anything to you?'

My mouth dropped open; my body became flooded with adrenaline and there were goosebumps all over my skin. A tear ran down my face as I replied, 'Yes. Yes, they do.'

There was no denying that something seemingly unexplainable (in words, anyway) was happening. It was clear to me that reiki had begun to release something deeper in me that I was never able to shift on my own. It was as if somebody had reached their hands deep into the cells of my body and given them a shake. Like flakes in a snow globe, my long-suppressed emotions were now released and floating around my body – finally free to be processed.

My scepticism about these so-called alternative therapies was well and truly disappearing into the distance. I would later share my experience with Syd, and as much as he found it interesting and supported everything I was doing, he still thought it was all a bit 'woo-woo'. Unlike me, he was extremely resistant to exploring his emotions any further than conversations with me; what I didn't know at the time was that there was a volcano of emotions lying dormant that would erupt a few years later. Like most people, I think he was too scared to face the negative feelings that were trapped in his subconscious – what the psychologist Carl Jung referred to as our 'shadow self'. It was too overwhelming. As the saying goes, you can lead a horse to water, but you cannot make him drink– and Syd was a stubborn old mule. I knew I had to honour his journey, however he chose to move through it, but I still insisted on trying to yank him as hard as I could to the water trough, often failing to make him take a drink, even when I dunked his head in.

One experience he had that year, however, did open him up from the inside out. He would refer to this as his 'awakening'.

It was 16th January 2016, a cold winter's day. It was snowing. After his morning cup of coffee, Syd decided to take a walk alongside the canal, close to his home– a walk he'd taken many times before. But he would describe this particular day as one of those beautiful picture-perfect days, like a scene you might see on an old-fashioned Christmas card. As he set foot on the crisp new snow, leaving fresh imprints behind him, out of nowhere he was overcome with an overpowering sense of joy, gratitude, and aliveness. He would describe it to me later as being just like the climactic scene in the Charles Dickens classic *A Christmas Carol*, when Ebenezer Scrooge experiences his redemption and exclaims on Christmas Day morning, 'I am light as a feather, I am happy as an angel, I am as merry as a schoolboy.'

He said all he could feel was happiness and pure love in his heart – as if it would burst in that very moment. He no longer hated his cancer; he thanked it for waking him up.

To some, this would sound strange; of course, this didn't mean he wanted everyone to get cancer in order to wake up, or that if he had the opportunity to be rid of the cancer, he wouldn't take it – not at all. What he meant was put beautifully by the great spiritual teacher Ram Dass who, following a devastating stroke, said, 'I don't wish you the stroke, but I wish you the grace from the stroke.' (Taken from the Netflix documentary *Going Home*).

Syd was compelled to write down his feelings in a notebook – something he had never done before. He would describe it as the day he realised he needed to follow his true desires – that he needed to listen to his heart. He wrote: 'Let spirit in and the whole universe is offered to you. The day I walked down that snowy canal was the day I went from being the seeker to the seer.'

It was a profound moment for him, and as I witnessed the change in him, I knew at the deepest level that this shift in his awareness was what brought us those miracle scan results that year.

CHAPTER ELEVEN: COMING HOME

When things fall apart in your life, you feel as if your whole world is crumbling. But actually, it's your fixed identity that's crumbling.
Pema Chodron

SO CLOSE, YET SO FAR

It was 20th July 2016. It was mid-afternoon and I had just arrived in the car park at the Royal Adelaide Hospital. Although it was freezing outside, I was sweating by the time I reached the small training room at the back of the emergency department. My heavy winter coat, extra layers and bags weighed heavily on my shoulders as I tried to wrestle my hair out of my face. I kicked the door open, then darted forward to avoid it smacking my backside as I entered. I began preparing my education session for a group of emergency nurses who were due to arrive any minute. It was my last session for the day, and I could feel myself beginning to wind down for the week; my holidays were fast approaching.

After many months of deliberation, we had finally booked a trip back to the UK. The time was right, and everything felt aligned. I was full of excitement about the trip and was desperate to see Syd again. We were due to attend Rick's brother's wedding in August, and my eleventh nephew had just been welcomed into the world. But overshadowing all of this joy was my grandma's declining health. My beloved Ganky's wife was now ninety-four years old and had already cheated death on several occasions; she had come so close just seven months earlier that I even wrote to her to say my final goodbye, convinced I would never see her again. But she shocked everyone, including the doctors, when she bounced back. 'She's hanging on for me,' I thought. But on that Wednesday afternoon as I glanced down at my phone and saw the word 'Mum' flashing up on the screen, my heart sank. There was only one reason she would be calling me at this time of day, and I just knew it wasn't going to be good news. With my stomach churning, I quickly answered the call.

'She's gone . . . I'm so sorry, Kay,' my mum said, fighting back her tears.

I couldn't believe it. The timing felt so cruel; I was just one week away from being reunited with her. I was devastated. As I hung up the phone, I wiped away my tears, took a deep breath and, rather than pack up and go home, I dug deep, swung the door open with the biggest smile I could muster, and welcomed the group of nurses who had been waiting patiently to start their training session. I spent the next forty-five minutes on autopilot.

A TOAST

Unlike our previous trip to the UK over five years earlier, and despite my grandma's death, this one was filled with joy, happiness, and finally a sense of togetherness on both sides of the family. My feelings during this trip caught me completely off guard. Out of nowhere, thoughts began to run through my mind about moving back home. I hadn't ever entertained the idea before, but I knew these were just thoughts. Theory was one thing; the reality of a move back home was quite another. The practicalities seemed impossible. We had good jobs which we both loved. We had a house, cars, dogs, and everything else that comes with that. Our entire life was now on the other side of the world. And not only that, but by now our boys had spent more of their lives in Australia than they had in the UK, so the transition – I thought – would just be too much for them. But whatever my thoughts about it at the time, the universe was going to keep nudging me and sending me signs.

One afternoon during that trip, these thoughts became impossible to ignore. We had arranged to meet up with all my family at my brother Ben's house. The sun was shining; it was a stunning English summer's day, the sort of day I would dream of but which rarely happened due to the unpredictable British weather. One thing's for sure: no one in the UK takes a day like that for granted. The birds were singing, the flowers were in full bloom, and as I heard the neighbours' lawnmowers humming away, I could smell the sweetness of the freshly cut grass hovering in the air. Every sound and smell transported me to my childhood. I knew this feeling. It was unconditional love. It was a wonderful feeling; it felt infinite.

As we all gathered in the garden, Syd arrived with his son. We embraced, both beaming from ear to ear. Here we were, together again, like peas and carrots. And now we were right back where we started: home. Not only that, but he was feeling good, he looked great, and we felt so much hope for his future. I stood proudly watching as my youngest nephews played on the swings, giggling and shouting for the older kids to push them higher.

As the afternoon continued, I was in a bubble of love, and I didn't want it to end. Cradling my glass of Prosecco, I walked over to the garden bench to sit with my brothers and Rick. As I glanced across the table, I noticed Syd plonk a bottle of wine right in the centre. *Could it be . . . ?* Yes, it was! True to his word, he'd kept that bottle of 2009 John's Blend Shiraz since his visit to us two years earlier. He proudly poured a glass for each of us and as he raised a toast, I could see the joy on his face from knowing that his plan had worked. We were home, and the seed he'd planted was beginning to grow.

GOODBYES

As I put my arms around Syd one last time before walking across the car park, I couldn't help but feel a sense of smugness, knowing I would see him again in just three months' time. We had just left our final meal together – a

Sunday roast at the local pub – before my return to Australia. We were due to fly out in the next few days, and never did I imagine that I would feel this way about leaving everyone.

I had been convinced before our arrival that I would be desperate to get back to the land down under, but this time it just wasn't the case. Despite Syd having flights booked to travel to Australia in November and my excitement about his visit, I couldn't ignore the pain of leaving everyone else once again. It felt like I was back in 2007 all over again. I couldn't hold back the tears as I bent down and planted a gentle kiss on my newborn nephew's tiny head as he lay snuggled in his car seat. The exact same scene from almost ten years earlier still haunted me – when I'd kissed my other nephew, Jack, on the head in his car seat before saying goodbye. It was all too eerily similar. A beautiful bond I had created, and here I was breaking it once again, with another nephew. I had no idea when I would see him again, or whether he would even know who I was. The sacrifices that came with living so far away from those I loved suddenly no longer felt worth it. As morbid as it sounds, I began to add up how many times I would likely see my parents again before they died. Even if they both had a good innings, it would be a maximum of five more visits. It just seemed ludicrous and totally unacceptable when I thought of it this way, but it was the harsh reality. As I continued to ponder and reflect during our journey to the hotel near Manchester Airport, I could sense the low-vibe energy coming from Rick and the boys. There was a distinct heaviness in the car.

'I don't want to go home, Mum. I want to stay here with everyone else,' Taylor said, with his head hanging down, as we sat beside the pool area in the hotel grounds.

'I know, darling, it's not easy. I get it. But we can't just upend our lives again. It's not that simple,' I said, trying my hardest to acknowledge his feelings but knowing I couldn't fix it for him in that moment.

We try to do that far too much as parents. We try to protect them from everything and anything that we think will cause them pain – of course we do; it's natural when we love them so much. But often we can unknowingly open them up to more pain and suffering in the long term. As a parent, I've learnt that it's important for our children to experience adversity in life, and that we should never try and sugar-coat life for them, however painful it is. Wherever possible, we must stay authentic and tell them the truth. If we lie to them – even if it's to protect them – they eventually learn not to trust us. We have to teach them that pain is inevitable, but it's what we do with that pain that matters. We don't have to suffer – that part is optional.

As we settled down for the night in our family room at the hotel, I picked up my phone and tapped on my Facebook app. There at the top of my news feed was a photo of my friend Brydie, one of the girls I had forged a friendship with through the Unicorn Foundation. She was a young mum in her early thirties, with a husband and two beautiful young boys, and she had been diagnosed a few years earlier with neuroendocrine cancer.

Before I left the UK, I had paid her a spur-of-the-moment visit. She had been extremely unwell following some gruelling back surgery and chemotherapy which had then led to complications. I knew I was going to be away for a month, so it felt right to go and see her before I left. I gently knocked on the door – just enough to be heard but not too loud as to startle her. I watched through the glass door as her blurry silhouette shuffled its way towards me. After a few minutes, she finally opened the door. 'I'm sorry I look like shit. I haven't even had a shower yet. Please excuse the mess!' she said, slightly embarrassed.

'No need to apologise,' I quickly replied, shocked that she would even think I cared about the state of her appearance or her house.

I followed her into the bedroom and watched as she struggled her way back onto the bed. Every movement she made seemed to be a herculean effort but, being so fiercely independent, she wouldn't accept any help. I slipped off my shoes and sat at the end of the bed, facing her, with my legs crossed. We sat and talked for about ten minutes. I don't really remember exactly what we talked about, but it was what she said before I left that stuck with me. As I noticed her fatigue quickly taking over, I could see she needed to rest, so I politely excused myself, saying I needed to get back to work; I knew she would never tell me to leave. As we said our goodbyes, she leant across the bed, put her hand on top of mine, and looked at me as if she was about to tell me something serious. She said, 'You go and have a wonderful time with your brother. Enjoy your time with your family – and remember, family is all that matters.'

As I stared at her photo on Facebook that evening in the hotel, the tears began to stream down my face as I slowly read the words announcing her death to the world. I remembered her poignant words to me; they suddenly sounded like a call to action.

SUPERHERO

By the time November 2016 came around, and following Syd's incredible scan results, everyone suddenly perceived me as the answer to Syd's prayers, as if I were some sort of guardian angel bestowing miracle after miracle upon him. I can remember feeling an incredible amount of pressure to 'fix him' and be the one who saved his life. What I didn't realise at the time was the damage that it was doing to my psyche.

My false self continued to trick me into believing that the only way to survive and to be loved was to save everyone else – to keep them happy. I was still trapped in the role of the 'fixer'. Everyone saw me as the superhero, flying in to save the day; it would even become my nickname at work, 'the superhero of wound care', complete with an animated sticker on top of my laptop. This led to me putting an enormous amount of pressure on myself to perform. Although it was just a joke, my ego didn't see it that way. I latched on to the label I had been given. I was proud of it. It made me feel loved and accepted. But what I couldn't see was that I was so busy trying to save everyone else, I forgot about me. And I was drowning.

BIRTHDAY CARD

'So let me ask you this,' Syd said as he sat on my kitchen bench, drinking a cup of tea.

I could tell he was about to ask me some sort of deep, profound question. We had reached a stage where neither of us could tolerate superficial conversations, and nothing was off the table as far as subject matter went.

'If you had the choice to enter one of two doors, and behind one of them was a paradise island with beautiful sunshine, palm trees, endless beauty, and behind the other door was a dreary, cold, and uninviting place, but all of the people you loved were there, which would you choose?'

I paused – only for a moment. 'I'd choose the door that led to the people I love, of course, hands down.'

'So why are you still here?' he said. 'How long are you going to keep this up for?'

I stared at him for a moment, dumbfounded. He'd stopped me in my tracks, and I had no response for him. It was so simple. Why *was* I still here?

Then, out of nowhere, I blurted out a comment with a level of vulnerability that surprised even me at the time. The iron mask well and truly slipped. 'I'm scared that if we go back, Rick won't be happy and he might leave me.'

'So what if he does?' he replied flippantly.

He was so matter-of-fact in his response that initially it irritated me. But then, as I started to consider what he had said, I realised there was something I needed to explore further within myself. I started to wonder: 'What if Rick does leave me? Why would I want to cling on to something if it's not real or true? And why do I feel as if I am not enough without him?'

It was like Syd had held a mirror uncomfortably close to my face that day and forced me to look deep into my soul and question everything I thought I knew. I didn't know it then, but this was the first time I caught a glimpse of my co-dependency. I didn't have words for it then – but there was definitely a subtle awareness.

In the months following Syd's return to the UK, I continued to skirt around the idea of leaving Australia and returning home. I would start to talk about the prospects loosely with colleagues at work, and with my friends and family. But every time we talked about it, the practicalities of it all just seemed so overwhelming. I was still living in fear. I was too scared to commit; I just wasn't ready to bet all my chips on black when there was still a chance I might land on red. But that niggling feeling inside me wouldn't subside. If I'm being brutally honest, I was waiting for a nudge. I was doing what most of us do when there is a difficult decision to be made: I wasn't deciding anything – but that, in and of itself, is a decision. I had decided to sit painfully in limbo, attempting to live two parallel lives, one inside my head and one inside my heart. And then the push I needed finally arrived.

I received a birthday card from Syd. He had never sent me a birthday card – well, not as an adult, anyway. He didn't like birthdays; in his words, he thought they were stupid. He couldn't understand why anyone would think being born was an achievement worth celebrating. So you can imagine my surprise when on my thirty-eighth birthday a card arrived in the mail from him. It said: 'To Sister Kay, come home, Universal Love, my spirit needs you xx'.

As my warm tears spilt down my cheeks, the decision was made without any hesitation. It had been taken out of my hands. It was the nudge I had been waiting for. We were going home, and this time it was final.

UNRAVELLING

I had romanticised about our return to the UK for almost six months. All the birthdays and Christmases we would no longer miss, all the support of family and friends I had longed for, particularly in a crisis – something I had missed deeply for over ten years. But most of all, I would have endless time to spend with my little brother. It would be a dream come true.

In hindsight I can see that I was, in many ways, peering through rose-tinted glasses. I was foolishly reimagining the years I had missed out on, and somehow believed I could drop right back where I left off, as if nothing had changed. It was so appealing: slipping back into my old life – safe, warm, and comfortable. I had made the mistake once again of thinking that by changing the outside I could fix the inside, that in some way all of life's challenges would be magically resolved the minute we were reunited with everyone back on British soil. It was a fairytale I had told myself, and I genuinely believed it. And to make matters worse, both Syd and I were secretly resting all our hopes for his survival on my return. He was waiting for the superhero to fly in.

Arriving home, I was ill prepared for the extreme change in the environment around me and the fast-paced lifestyle I was about to be thrown back into. It was as if my nervous system had been arrested. I felt immediately exposed and under attack. It was like trying to gently place my foot on a spinning roundabout, and I was being dragged under – fast. I felt completely out of control. What had we done?

As my inner turmoil raged on, it began to express itself in the form of physical symptoms. I suffered with a chest infection that I couldn't shift for over six weeks, closely followed by a nasty stomach infection with Campylobacter that ripped through my gut like a hurricane. I was out of action for almost three months, on and off, which left me feeling depressed, with a side order of anxiety.

Syd's health had taken a nosedive, too. By the time I arrived home, just three weeks before Christmas, he was so unwell that he was unable to leave his bed, and refused to see anyone other than my parents, me, and Rick. His cancer was causing further complications, and his body had become a shitstorm of unwanted hormones and chemicals. He was literally fighting for his life, and the only way out was more surgery – this time to remove his adrenal glands. Over time, doctors had tried to control the cancer-induced imbalances in his body with a number of medications, but they were no longer working. They had no choice but to cut the problem off at the source.

The adrenal glands are two small glands that sit just above your kidneys. Although they're only very small, they have a vital role in producing a number of hormones in the body, including steroid hormones, adrenaline, and noradrenaline, which are essential for balancing bodily functions such as blood pressure, heart rate, blood sugars, metabolism, and the stress response. Ordinarily, in the absence of disease, the adrenal glands are perfectly able to delicately balance the levels of these hormones that are released into the bloodstream. However, in Syd's case, his disease was causing disruption to this fragile balance, and mayhem had ensued. The outrageous amount of the stress hormone cortisol flooding his body was slowly but surely killing him. Surgery wasn't something he had to think about for long. Quite simply, if he didn't have them removed, he would die.

During those first few months after arriving home, I was struggling to find my place. I couldn't seem to get a handle on anything; I had lost my flow. I had taken a job working back in medical recruitment again – the same job I'd left ten years earlier when we left the UK – but it quickly became apparent this was a huge mistake. I had opted for security again – my comfort zone. I was back under my rock where it was safe. Had I learnt nothing?

As time marched on, the stress and feeling of being at odds with myself became too great a burden to bear. I arrived home from work one evening in floods of tears. Rick sat and listened as I explained exactly what was happening. Without hesitation, he told me to leave my job immediately and take some time off. I had no desire to argue with him – I knew deep down that was what I needed to do. I was just waiting once again for that magic permission slip.

I would spend the next three months unemployed yet completely free – free of the shackles I had felt wrapped so tightly around my entire being. I was finally relieved of the stress and terrible discomfort of forcing myself to do something for a living that I no longer cared about. I was hungry for meaning and purpose, and medical recruitment was most definitely not it. I may not have known exactly what I wanted to do with my life at that point – which was frightening – but I did know exactly what I didn't want. I didn't want to do anything that did not align with my true self any longer. I'd had enough of insulting my soul. I was making myself sick.

Despite this new-found sense of freedom, there was no denying that it brought with it a feeling of being lost at sea. I had to get comfortable with not knowing, with the mystery of it all. I had to let go and see what happened. Just like getting stuck in a rip in the ocean – the only way to get out is not to struggle or swim against it but to surrender and float with the current, and it will eventually bring you back to shore. My false self was screaming out for safety, security, and the illusion of control. I had to ignore it, sit tight, and stay open to all possibilities.

Over the next three months, Syd and I spent every moment we could together. He was slowly recovering from the surgery he'd had in February, and other than some spells of fatigue, he seemed fine. Or at least that's what he had us all believe. We visited all our childhood haunts, taking long walks and lazy lunches in what turned out to be one of the hottest summers on record, the summer of 2018. The country was gripped by World Cup fever.

One day in May, we took a trip to Malham, a tiny village just a few miles from our childhood home and where we went to primary school together. It was a place we both loved – we called it our happy place. You could almost hear the echoes of the past in the fields that surrounded us. We walked for around three miles, taking in the scenery, talking and laughing all the way. Knowing what I know now, I'm in awe of his determination to show up for days like that when he was in such a tremendous amount of pain. As we headed back towards the car, I noticed he looked tired and a little out of breath. I suggested we rest for a while in the shade of a tree, close to where the car was parked. I unwrapped my hoodie from around my waist and laid it on the lush green grass beneath my feet. As I slipped off my sandals, I noticed the dappling shadows of the tree, which seemed to stretch out far and wide in front of us – on display as if only for our pleasure. As I breathed in the fresh summer's air and gently closed my eyes, I knew in that moment that no matter what happened, we would always be together.

In August 2018, life was continuing to happen around me. By now I had taken another job, driven by the need to pay the bills. It wasn't the job of my dreams, but it was close to home, and I liked the company ethos. The job would only last three months, but during that time, I experienced a nervous breakdown. The years of wearing the iron mask, carrying the load, hiding my grief, resenting my husband, and opting to escape reality finally caught up with me in the most explosive way possible, catching me and everyone I love off guard.

I knew something was coming. I had predicted it when I wrote in my journal on 1st August 2018:

> *Something weird is happening to me. I am anxious, emotional, paranoid, and insecure. I am not coping with life and every day feels like a struggle. I feel completely out of alignment.*

Then, just a few weeks later– during a family camping trip, and following an alcohol-induced argument– I lost control of myself in the scariest way possible and physically attacked my sister-in-law and my husband in a fit of rage.

It has been said that unresolved grief often expresses itself as anger. In her book *Get Over It*, Iyanala Vanzant lists three fears that lead to anger:

1. Fear of losing control
2. Fear of not being loved
3. Fear of being helpless.

What I was experiencing at this time was a total loss

of control and feeling utterly helpless. It still shocks me as I write about it now, as if I'm watching events that happened to someone else. I became completely dissociated from myself. It was as if someone else had taken over my physical body and I was watching it all unfold, horrified. I had projected every part of me that was dying on the inside directly outwards and towards two of the people closest to me.

The days and weeks that followed that night were perhaps some of the scariest, loneliest, and most torturous I have ever experienced. I felt deep shame and embarrassment about my actions and wasn't sure whether I could ever be forgiven, or even forgive myself. How could I have done this to someone I love? What was happening to me?

This turned out to be the beginning of my journey inwards. I couldn't play at this thing called life any more. I couldn't ignore what was happening; I was OK with hurting myself, but the minute I started hurting the people I loved . . . then I knew something had to change. I needed help. I had to be brave and start being more honest with my own family, so I boldly told my brothers and my parents what had happened and that I no longer recognised myself. Although shocked, they were extremely supportive and told me they were there for me no matter what. They didn't judge me or abandon me – which had always been my fear. When my mum said, 'Sometimes, darling, we all need help. It's OK,' I suddenly felt genuine relief that I didn't need to hide my feelings any longer. It was OK to not be OK. I felt safe.

I think I had spent so many years wrapped up in Rick's

depression that I didn't think I was allowed to fall apart. I had witnessed this same pattern in my parents many years earlier. Following my mum's illness in the nineties, my dad had a nervous breakdown. He had carried the load – trying to juggle running a home, growing a business, and raising four children while my mum remained emotionally and physically unavailable for many years. Eventually, when my mum started to show signs of recovery, the balance tipped, and my dad mentally fell off a cliff. He would admit years later to thoughts of suicide. Like me, he too sought help and saw his local GP and a homeopath, and thankfully, he made it to the other side. But many don't, so I believe sharing these experiences is so important. It doesn't make us weak or 'less than'; in fact, I have come to realise that those who suffer with depression, anxiety or any other mental illness are often the strongest people I know.

One day, early in September of 2018, I finally plucked up the courage to call my local GP and make an appointment. As I sat in her office just a few days later, I began to tell her exactly what had been happening. What did I have to lose? With my chin wobbling like a newborn baby's and my eyes leaking profusely, I couldn't hold in my emotions any longer. I let loose, and suddenly the pain and hurt I had been carrying around with me for many years gushed out like a tsunami. After several minutes I caught myself thinking, 'She must think I'm so dramatic. Other people have way more worries than I do. How embarrassing'. I sat back in my chair, took a deep breath, and waited for her response. I was desperately hoping she would understand. That's all we really want, I think: to be understood, to feel we belong – to be connected.

She looked at me sympathetically and calmly said, 'It's OK. You're going to be OK. You're having a nervous breakdown and suffering from intense anxiety and depression. You're not alone, and it's understandable after all that you've been through and are still going through.'

I realised there, in that moment, that I wasn't on my own. And I knew I deserved to feel better. For that to happen, though, I needed to be gentler on myself. For as long as I could remember, I had been the strong one, the perfectionist, the control freak, the achiever, the winner. I had to begin the process of reframing my thoughts about myself – changing some of those labels, questioning and relearning some of those belief patterns that had become so familiar to me. Although reluctant at first, I accepted a prescription for a course of antidepressants, and I was put on the waiting list for counselling, which I welcomed. Unfortunately, as is now common with the mental health system in the UK (and is probably similar in other countries too), the waiting list was long – twelve weeks.

I knew I didn't have twelve weeks to wait. I was struggling to function – it took all of my energy just to be able to get out of bed every morning. So I decided to do whatever I could to help myself. I drew on all the knowledge I had gained from years of reading, and started to put some of those learnings into practice. I had the knowledge; now I had to act.

I picked up my journal and wrote a list of everything that was bothering me – all my worries, concerns, and deepest fears.

Perhaps if I got them all out on paper, they wouldn't seem quite so scary. Next, I would follow this up with a list of realistic actions I could take to do something about minimising or erasing these fears. These two lists were critical to start the healing process, and they involved a great deal of honesty – if I couldn't be honest, I knew they would be rendered useless. Finally, I wrote a list of affirmations. I remembered all I'd learnt from Louise Hay about how effective they had been in her life – the same could work for me, right? I would read these affirmations every day, repeating them over and over. Some days I would believe them, other days I wouldn't. I quickly became aware of how easy it was for my false self to hijack my true self. I had to be persistent in rewiring my old thought patterns.

About a month later, the medication was helping, and I was feeling much stronger. I felt like the dark cloud over my head was lifting, and decided it was time to start rebuilding my relationship with my sister-in-law. I sent her a text message asking to meet one evening at the local pub (no alcohol involved), and she agreed.

I don't think I've ever been as nervous as I was that night. My adrenaline was racing, because I was fearful that there would be confrontation on her part. Like me, she has a fiery nature, and I was convinced that she no longer loved me. I had let her down, and I feared that what I had done would be unforgivable. I was prepared for an angry tirade, and I was willing to surrender to it all and accept whatever came. My guard was completely down and all I had left was to be completely myself – the rawest, truest version.

As I sobbed uncontrollably, I started to explain what had been happening to me. All of it. Her body language and energy seemed to shift. There was a sudden calmness. It reminded me of a scene in the movie *Hook* with Robin Williams, who played Peter Banning, a burnt-out, stressed-out, uncaring father who has forgotten who he really is. He has become so wrapped up in life that he has forgotten his true identity: Peter Pan. The Lost Boys tease and taunt him, unable to believe that he's the real Peter Pan, until a beautiful moment when the youngest of them notices something and moves closer to him. The boy ushers Peter down to his level and lifts his hands up to his face. He gently stretches the skin on his face, and suddenly he catches a glimpse of the real Peter. He says, 'Oh, there you are, Peter!' He's able to see beyond the façade and deep into Peter's being. To me, this is true love for another: being able to look beyond the current situation – no matter how terrible – and see someone for who they truly are. That day, my sister-in-law saw me. The real me. The messy, fucked-up, vulnerable me. Not the well-put-together, organised, perfectionist me. As we hugged one another tightly in that pub car park, I knew the healing had begun. It's only recently – almost three years later – that we've talked openly about that horrible evening in August again. I am certain now that time, patience, love and being willing to be vulnerable is what saved our relationship.

As painful as it was, my unravelling came at just the right time. I needed to build my strength, as there was a runaway train up ahead, heading straight for us.

CHAPTER TWELVE: THE GREAT PRETENDER

One of the greatest tragedies in life is to lose your own sense of self and accept the version of you that is expected by everyone else.
K.L. Toth

Oh yes, Syd was the great pretender. He had been pretending to everyone – for years. Even, at times, to me. He had been living a life that he felt wasn't his own, but he didn't know how to talk to anyone about it. He never sought help, or even acknowledged there were problems. He had mountains of repressed guilt, shame, unhappiness, and fear which he carried around with him. He had avoided it all – pushing it down, hoping it would go away – but as he would later tell me, with his hand resting on his chest, 'I've grown myself a tumour instead.'

What he had been hiding wasn't some deep, dark, terrible secret – that's the saddest thing. What he'd been hiding was simply the fact that he felt like his whole life had been wrong. Every decision he'd made in life beyond the age of twenty-one had been for other people, based on what he thought others expected of him. He was locked in the invisible cage, where he had slowly gathered all the things he thought he should have but which were never going to make him truly happy. This would lead to frustration, anger and resentment towards others and himself. Eventually, he lost trust in himself. The career he chose, the marriage and the family he wasn't ready for, the place he chose to live – all of it was misaligned with his heart and soul. He was constantly at odds with himself. And, over time, this proved to be destructive.

Despite his spiritual insights in 2016, he continued to hide his deep, unprocessed fear about his life, his cancer, and death – unwilling to completely let his guard down even with those closest to him. I would watch on as his egoic mind would gain strength and hold him hostage in the worst ways. He tried so hard to conceal the genuine depth of pain and hurt he was experiencing and, like many people who suffer, he found it easier to cope by 'putting a face on' and making light of it – and my God, could he make us all laugh, even at the strangest times! He refused to drag the mood down or be a burden to anyone.

I recall replying to a message he sent me to say that he'd been struggling emotionally after I'd visited him one day at the hospice. When I asked him why he hadn't said anything at the time, he responded by saying, 'no one wants a crybaby.' As I read his message, I felt like someone had just squeezed my heart. I could physically feel his pain and sadness. On another occasion, during the final weeks of his life, he sent me a message saying, 'I'm really worried about Mum, I'm not sure how she's coping with all of this.' He was always concerned with our feelings and not his own. I think all too often as a society we celebrate people who sacrifice everything for other people. To be selfless is seen as a highly admirable trait – 'isn't she amazing,' we say, 'she's so selfless, always thinking about others before herself.' But looking at the word itself – self-less– we become self-less. We are less than ourselves. When we continually give ourselves to others, we often lose ourselves in the process. And it happens unconsciously. It happened to Syd, and it was happening to me.

My brother's determination – or stubbornness, depending which way you look at it – meant that he would continue to keep up appearances. It was his way of surviving, his way of coping. His brain had tricked him. He was fooled into thinking that was his safe place. But the irony was, it became his living nightmare. Lurking below his impressive display of strength, his suppressed emotions were silently destroying his insides. Then in October 2018, following a near-death experience, he burst open like a jack-in-the-box. He started to unravel.

WHAT IF IT WAS ALL WRONG?

Up until Syd's diagnosis, I had rarely contemplated death. As a society, particularly in Western countries, we tend to avoid it. It's considered a taboo subject, as if we will somehow hasten our own death if we even mention it. We tell ourselves it won't happen to us. But it will. And it does, every single minute of every single day. It's one of the two things in life that are certain– change and death – which are in many ways the same.

My earliest memory of contemplating my own mortality is from when I was around age nine. The memory is a little sketchy, but I can vaguely remember sitting in the back of the family car, on our way home from our grandparents' house – it was late at night, and I was hanging over the back seat, looking through the rear window, watching the rain lash down. There must have been a conversation between my parents about someone who had recently died. I can recall vividly a sense of darkness and horror descending on me as I considered the fact that if I died, I would never exist again on this earth. 'Is that it?' I thought. 'Do you just die and there's nothing? Just blackness, forever?' The feeling was so overwhelming that all I could do to avoid the horrible feeling in my tummy was to push it away and ignore it. And for the next thirty years, that's exactly what I did.

But I've come to realise that without facing our own mortality, we run the risk of leading a life half-lived, always on guard, fooling ourselves into thinking we are somehow immortal. We think we have all this time available to us, when in fact we have a finite amount: on average, just four thousand weeks. So we save the expensive outfits for special occasions, we wait until next week, next year to finish the passion project, we don't call our parents, we don't tell or show those closest to us that we love them often enough, never realising that nothing is in our control, and it can all end in an instant. It's all an illusion.

If we're not careful, we can end up with a long list of

regrets. In Bronnie Ware's book *The Five Regrets of the Dying*, she outlines that there are common regrets among all of us. Bronnie is a nurse who cared for patients during their final weeks of life. During her career, she came to notice a pattern emerging among her patients in terms of their regrets in life. She decided to document them in the hope that others could learn from their shared wisdom and avoid having the same regrets. As I sat with my brother during those final twelve weeks of his life, I witnessed the exact same pattern emerging, and it was truly heartbreaking to watch. And just like Bronnie, my hope is that my sharing our story will help others to avoid asking themselves 'What if my life was all wrong?'.

The number one regret of the dying is 'I wish I'd had the courage to live a life true to myself, not the life others expected of me'. This was painfully true for Syd. In October 2018 – when everything came crashing down, followed quickly by that final scan in November – he suddenly gave up his role of the Great Pretender. As he began to crumble physically, he was no longer able to bear the weight of the mask he was wearing, and as it fell away it revealed everything that had been hiding underneath. It was a confusing time for him, and heartbreaking to watch. All his repressed emotions were now fully exposed, and as they bubbled to the surface, they brought a tidal wave of tears and hurt. There were moments of liberation and freedom, but they were quickly followed by anger and frustration. It was as if every resentment and disappointment he had been harbouring on the inside finally burst through his thick outer shell. As Wayne Dyer once said, 'when you squeeze an orange it's the juice that comes out' – not apple juice or carrot juice. It's the same with people: when you put them under immense pressure, what comes out is what's on the inside. Trying to make light of the situation, I even gave him a nickname: the angry Peperami© (if you don't know or remember the advert, look it up).

The truth was, it was painful, scary, and unsettling to see this person I knew and loved fighting with his false-self. The anger he projected seemed, at times, to be directed towards other people – but he knew, and I knew, that the only person he was angry with was himself. He would shoot me knowing glances during meetings with doctors and the palliative care team nurses – nodding for me to speak on his behalf, even openly verbalising one afternoon sitting on my mum's couch, 'Speak to my sister – she knows exactly what I'm thinking and feeling, she will explain it to you.'

His frustration reached an all-time high as he realised he had become the equal sum of the choices he'd made. Now he wanted to choose again – and the tragedy was, he couldn't. He had run out of options.

Despite the anger and frustration, there were moments of pure bliss and happiness. They existed where they often do – in simple moments. I had many sleepovers at the hospital and the hospice. We would stay up watching trash TV and talking into the early hours of the morning. We ate crap, drank wine, and laughed – a lot. One afternoon, I picked him up from the hospital and raced his wheelchair through the hospital corridors, accompanied by my best rally car impersonation. His face was beaming, and we both laughed like little kids. There was also this wonderful sense of freedom he seemed to experience when he had no choice but to let go – he suddenly felt like he could be himself. He started to grow his hair out; he had worn it short and neat all of his adult life, then suddenly decided to let it go wild, and his natural curls made an appearance. He relished running his hands through it, and he would say, 'I feel like Bradley Cooper now,' with a cheeky grin.

Then one evening on our way back from St James's Hospital, following a meeting with his consultant (where there was never any good news), he suddenly directed me to a McDonald's close by and told me he wanted to try a Big Mac.

'What? You've never had a Big Mac?' I said, in shock.

'Nope – never. I feel like mixing it up a bit,' he said sarcastically. 'I want to know what all the bloody fuss is about. They can't be that good, can they?'

I pulled in and switched the engine off. As I sat back and watched him get out of the car outside a grubby McDonald's on the outskirts of Bradford, I remember thinking 'How on earth did I end up here?' – I had left paradise for this. And yet there was truly nowhere on earth I would rather have been in that moment. We quickly ordered our food and as we sat down with our nutritious delights, I watched on expectantly as he sank his teeth into the famous burger.

'Not bad, not bad at all. I can't believe I've been missing out all of these years,' he said, glancing out of the window.

As the tears began to sneak their way out of the corners

of his eyes, I knew this wasn't about a stupid Big Mac; he was grieving for all the choices he hadn't made and the future he no longer had.

Around the same time, and after months of resistance, he finally accepted that he could no longer live on his own. He had spent years living alone in an apartment just ten minutes away from our parents. He always claimed he was happy being alone, and there was no doubt he loved his solitude, but in time he had unknowingly closed himself off in many ways, and his stubborn nature would never allow him to admit that he was desperately lonely. Although it was uncomfortable for him to admit he needed help, once the decision was made and he moved in with Mum and Dad permanently, I could see a weight being lifted off his shoulders. He sent me a message during those first few weeks telling me it was the happiest he'd been since he was a child. He was on cloud nine, and for the first time in a long time I saw moments of joy dancing across his eyes. He was starting to enjoy the process of letting things go. I think he felt he had returned to safety – and with that, he was finally able to return to himself.

CHAPTER THIRTEEN: THE VOID

All forms of loss are a confrontation to the ego and
its survival mechanisms. All aspects of human life
are transient, so to cling to any aspect eventually
brings grief and loss. Each incident, however,
is an opportunity to search within for the source
of life, which is ever present, unchanging,
and not subject to loss or the ravages of time.
David R. Hawkins

Out of all the chapters in this book, this has been the hardest for me to write. But I have learnt that there can be no joy without suffering. We cannot have one without the other – it's the paradoxical way of life. We breathe in, then we breathe out; there is dark, then there is light; the tides rush in, then they rush out. Without the pain, we would never know bliss.

HOW DO YOU PREPARE FOR DEATH?

When my boys were born, there was an adage that people used to say to me: 'Babies don't come with an instruction manual'. And it's true – they don't. As a first-time mum, I often felt helpless and had no idea what I was doing. There may be all the books in the world promising to prepare you for the birth, the first months, the first years . . . but essentially, they all get thrown out of the nearest window once the baby arrives. I was not immune to this process, and to make matters worse, I had the added stress of becoming a mother at the tender age of twenty. I thought I was mature; I was not. All I had to help me through those first few months was advice from family and friends, but ultimately it came down to my maternal instincts.

I had known from the very moment Syd was born that I was going to be a mother. I was– and still am, in many ways– addicted to loving and being loved, and my mum had passed the maternal baton on to me. So, when Louis and Taylor were born, I fumbled my way through, like most new mothers, using a lot of trial and error; but in the end, it was my strong intuition and unconditional maternal love that made me a good mother, not the step-by-step instructions in a 'how to' book. Those steps are still useful, of course, and without them I would have been completely lost, but we often get too bogged down in the detail, obsessing over routines, and forget that our babies are not machines – and nor do we want them to be.

It's the same when it comes to death: we don't have a clue what we're doing, and we have to rely solely on our instincts. And to make things even more difficult, we don't prepare for death in the same way as we prepare for birth. Why is that? Why isn't it common practice to take breathing classes, or write a death plan? Why aren't we encouraged to read books on how to die well? Death is natural, after all, and it is an inevitable part of life, isn't it? Why do we wait until someone's funeral to tell them how we really feel about them? Why don't we do that when they're still here? Why do we tell people to rest in peace? Why can't they live in peace? We spend most of our lives avoiding the subject of death; I mean, it doesn't seem like a cheery conversation starter, does it? I think we have been taught from a young age (albeit unconsciously) to fear death. I often walk past our local funeral home and wonder to myself why everything is always black. The doors, the walls, the hearse, even the traffic cones they use to hold the parking space at the front are black. It all seems so uninviting – depressing, cold and, quite frankly, scary.

Where there is death, there is often silence. We are told that silence is respectful to the dead and their grieving families – but why? It has never made sense to me. Silence, in my experience – about anything – causes nothing but fear, shame and, eventually, more suffering. Why do we have to be silent around death? Are we scared that if we talk about it, we'll invite the grim reaper to our door? As I mentioned earlier, the problem is that we've created an illusion that we will live forever. We think it won't ever happen to us. We bury the idea away and avoid it at all costs. Until we can't.

As Syd's final weeks approached, I desperately wished I had a manual, or that I had some guidance on what to do, what to say, what to expect – I wished I had picked up that book of Ganky's years earlier and read what was on those pages. Had he found some guidance and comfort in there? I felt like I was rich in knowledge about life but knew very little about death. Syd and I had talked and even joked about death. Whenever the conversation came up, he would just say, 'We are all going to die – it's just I have a better idea of when my time is up. You could die tomorrow and not even know it.' And he was right. I would often think, 'If that's the case, then surely we should all be living with a conscious awareness that death is only ever a moment away? Maybe then we would live our lives more fully, instead of pretending we have all the time in the world?'

His outward approach to death was truly inspiring. But what others could not see was the fear and anxiety he kept well hidden. The hardest part was that we both always held a genuine belief that he could and would survive, even when all seemed lost; we were forever committed to the possibility of a miracle. But after that fateful scan in November, the jokes became fewer, and the reality we were facing together seemed to close in on us. It wasn't so much death itself that he was fearful of – we had both found comfort in our spiritual beliefs and deep faith – it was the perpetual fear of *how* he would die.

When he moved into the hospice permanently, not long after Christmas, he was given a questionnaire to fill in almost every day. As the nurse brought it in one afternoon and popped it down on his wheelie tray, he looked across at me and nodded towards the pen and paper. 'You fill it in for me – you know how I'm feeling. Go on,' he said, continuing to nod incessantly.

'Oh, go on then. Give it here,' I said, rolling my eyes. I started to read through the questions one by one, telling him what answer I would give and checking he was happy with it. He was a Virgo, after all – he needed to stay in control at all times. Most of the questions were practical and were essentially to monitor how far 'downhill' he was going each day. Then I read out question number eight: 'What are you most anxious about today?'

He shot a look at me, then looked at Mum and Dad, then burst into laughter and said, 'Dying, of course – what a stupid bloody question!'

We all erupted into laughter.

THE FIRST OF THE LASTS

As we approached Christmas 2018, we all knew it would be Syd's last, and I was determined to make it the best Christmas he'd ever had. By this stage, I was travelling over to see Syd most days, trying to juggle my time with him and my full-time work commitments as a medical rep on the road. I drove over one hundred and fifty miles most days. I was tired, but I didn't care – I had flicked on the autopilot switch. Rick would liken it to the scenes with Wallace and Gromit when Wallace uses the bed waking lever and instantly rises from the bed, ignoring all other distractions; my alarm would go off, or the phone would ring with another emergency call from Syd, and I would shoot up out of bed and be in my clothes and out the door within ten minutes flat. That continued for months. It didn't matter how exhausted I was – those months were all I had left with him, and I would make whatever sacrifice was necessary to be with him as often as I could. It's as if my brain would shut off any kind of future beyond the given moment; I had a job to do, and whatever happened after that could wait. I continued to be his voice with the doctors and nursing staff caring for him. I spoke on his behalf, I completed forms, organised meetings, made phone calls, and tried to do whatever I could to make sure he was assured at all times that he didn't need to fear anything— that his big sister was right there by his side. The reality was, of course, that I wasn't able to fix everything.

I arrived at my parents' house around twelve o'clock. It was 21st December 2018 – a special date in my diary. It was my Ganky's birthday. Every year when we were little kids, we would go to Grandma and Ganky's house for a buffet on his birthday. It was an annual tradition— and, being only four days away from the big day, we were beside ourselves with excitement about the impending visit from the big man, so it marked the start of the official countdown to Christmas. Syd and I shared fond memories of this day and would recall the warm, cosy house, the endless supply of Coca-Cola with slices of lemon, dry-roasted peanuts, tins of Quality Street, and After Eight mints. Gran would put on a wonderful spread, with enough food to feed the entire street.

The memories from this day were so special to me that every year since my Ganky had passed away in 1998 I continued to mark that date with either a special lunch or, when we lived in Australia, a picnic on the beach or by the lake. So this year would be no different. Finally, after eleven years apart, I could share this tradition with Syd.

He had only been home from the hospice for a few weeks and was being cared for by the palliative care team every day. He was on a cocktail of painkillers and steroids which were being drip-fed through permanent syringes attached to his thighs. I wondered if we would even make it out for lunch that day, but his determination once again astounded me. I ran up the stairs to his room, half expecting to see him in bed, but as I burst through the door, I was shocked to see he was standing, fully dressed and ready to go. I paused and looked at him for a moment, knowing the effort that must have gone into getting himself up that day. I smiled at him, letting him know just how proud I was.

'Do I look OK?' he said, with a concerned tone. I remember thinking he sounded like a child. I noticed he was wearing a thick, ribbed white jumper with a high collar – not something I had seen him in for a long time. It had a zip from the centre of his chest right up to his chin.

'Yes, you look great – very swish. I love that jumper – it suits you,' I said.

He lifted his hand up and placed it on his chest. 'Can you see it?' he said nervously, referring to the lump rising underneath.

My heart broke. 'No, no, not at all,' I quickly replied, eager to satisfy his worries.

'Right. Let's go then, knobhead,' he said with a wry smile.

It would be our last lunch out together – and I still don't know how he did it.

That year, we decided to celebrate Christmas on Christmas Eve. My parents did such an excellent job when we were little, by upholding traditions, that Christmas Eve became more exciting than Christmas Day. It was all about the anticipation. Every year it was tradition for Mum to dress the Christmas table in all its glory, prepare the turkey and all the trimmings . . . and after weeks of waiting, we could finally open the last door on the advent calendar. With the log burners roaring, we would enjoy special drinks and a variety of treats that had been kept in the kitchen cupboard, untouched, for most of December. When we were a little older, they would take us to midnight mass at the local church. Like any child, of course I was excited about the presents, but for me looking back (and even now), I know it was always about the love we shared as a family and the sense of togetherness and belonging. That's what made me happy. And never had that been truer than in 2018. Syd made a request for Dad to put the original Christmas tree up in the living room – the same one they'd had when we were born. This Christmas tree was my parents' first tree when they were married almost fifty years ago. It's now a small raggedy old thing, but somehow my parents have managed to preserve it all these years. It even comes complete with the handmade crackers and baubles we made in school. It's swarming with our childhood memories, a priceless antique, and it brought great comfort to us that year.

Christmas Eve 2018 was a beautiful day. It was a crisp -2ºC as we set off that morning, and there wasn't a cloud in the sky. It felt so Christmassy – it was perfect. We pulled up outside my parents' home and as Rick turned the engine off, I took a moment and glanced up at my brother's room. I knew it would be the last time I would do this – forever. I took a deep breath and as Rick put his hand on mine and gave it a comforting squeeze, I turned and stepped out of the car. I had to put my game face on; although we never avoided the reality of the situation, I wanted this day to be filled with laughter and joy. I was determined not to let sorrow get in the way.

'Merry Christmas, little brother,' I said with a big smile as I waltzed into his room. He was lying on the bed wearing his short-sleeved blue checked hoodie and light-blue jogging pants. I sat on the edge of the bed in my little black dress and shimmied my way across to give him a hug; as I closed my eyes and felt his slim frame, I was careful not to squeeze too hard. He was in pain every day – he very rarely showed it, but having witnessed the agony he sometimes couldn't hide, I was often reluctant to touch him for fear of setting it off in some way. The reality was that his pain would come out of nowhere and in different places, and it was never really under control.

'Bloody hell, you've curled your hair – it must be a special occasion!' he replied, acknowledging the importance of the day.

After dinner we exchanged gifts. I bought him Top Trumps, the card game we played as kids, and a special-edition glass, shaped like a reindeer's head from the famous film *National Lampoon's Christmas Vacation*. It even came with the replica Santa hat that Clark Griswold wore in the film. I bought eggnog for him to drink out of it so he could re-enact the scene – plus, I knew he'd never tried it before, and he had always wondered what it tasted like. Apparently not that great. Finally, I reached across the sofa and passed him a small box. The final gift I would ever give him. He carefully opened the box and lifted out two silver necklaces. They matched – the same small silver cross – and both were inscribed. He read the inscriptions aloud. On one, it read 'always with me' and on the other, 'always with you'. Without hesitation and with a sense of urgency in his voice, he asked me to put his necklace on straight away. I could see the comfort he instantly felt as his eyes softened and welled up. We both looked up, mirroring one another as our hands rested on our chests.

'I am always with you, and you will always be with me,' I firmly reassured him.

The day continued to play out exactly as I had planned. We ate, we drank, we laughed, we cried – I was lost in a haze of love, and Syd would later tell me it was the best Christmas he'd ever had. It seemed so cruel that it would be his last.

WHAT'S THE POINT?

'I feel like there's a train heading straight for me. I'm strapped to the train tracks, and I can hear the train, but no one can tell me when it's going to hit,' he said, looking at me for answers. 'What's the point?'

I had no answers for him. He was right. What was the point? He knew he was dying – we all knew he was dying –

yet he was kept alive in agonising pain for the remaining six weeks of his life, for no reason. We don't do this to our animals, so why do we do it to our fellow human beings? Syd was a practical man. He hated waste, so even the cost of keeping him alive was bothering him. Every time he took his pills, he would comment what a waste of money it all was. The drugs being drip-fed into his veins to keep him comfortable were just putting off the inevitable – and, more often than not, didn't even work.

One afternoon Clive, one of the palliative care doctors, came to speak with Syd. I sat holding his hand and listened. 'Syd, we can give you drugs to make you sleepier, but you need to understand that once you're asleep, we won't be able to bring you out of the sedation.'

We looked at each other, then looked back at him and with a gentle nod he agreed this was what he wanted. His pain had become unbearable and was the only reason he was distraught most days. He would often describe it to me as like a living nightmare. He likened it to the film *Avatar* – he would go to sleep, be able to run around and be free in his dreams, then wake up trapped in a body that was completely and utterly broken, unable to move. The mental torture was, at times, overwhelming for him.

I must point out here that I don't write so openly to shock or scare anyone – I write this because I made a promise to be Syd's voice and the voice of others going through something similar. The truth is important; others should feel they can speak up and be heard, no matter how difficult it may be.

There was too much 'looking away' going on, and there's too much skirting around the subject of assisted dying, mainly because the doctors fear they'll be sued for being seen to kill their patients. I'm certain these doctors feel exactly the same way that we do – they don't want to see their patients suffer. The stark reality, though, is that about seventeen per cent of terminally ill patients suffer the same way Syd did, and even one percent would be too many (statistic referenced in *Last Rights* by Sarah Wootton and Lloyd Riley.) Luckily, the laws are changing around the globe, and assisted dying has been back on the agenda in the UK – but the politics and bureaucracy surrounding the decisions are holding back the moral and ethical rights of every human being living and suffering terribly with a terminal illness. I am confident, though, that in the not-so-distant future, people in the same position as Syd will be given the option to end their lives when they choose to, thereby avoiding the endless, unnecessary suffering of not only themselves but their families, too. In the current system, we are robbing people of their right to die with dignity and peace. To me, this is unacceptable.

We are not all built the same – this I know to be true. Syd was made from what seemed like indestructible steel. He was like the Terminator. The doctors kept trying to shoot him down, but his body would just shake it off and get back up. His stubbornness was so ingrained and his brain so well trained that he carried on fighting subconsciously, even when he didn't want to. The doctors and nurses were baffled by his ability to stay conscious when he'd been given enough drugs to knock out not one but five elephants. The consultant stated that in his entire career as a palliative care doctor, he had never known any patient with such an indomitable will.

I would often enter his room quietly, trying not to disturb him, but as soon as I poked my head around the door, his head would spin around like a big tawny owl's, his curious eyes looking to see who was there. He refused to miss anything. He was still messaging me on WhatsApp every day, only stopping three days before he died. He seemed to be on a mission to prove to all of us that he could not be beaten. His innate competitive nature took over.

As children, it was hammered into our psyche to never, ever give up. And while this is an admirable trait – and the reason I have overcome many challenges in my own life – it can also become a curse. What we resist, persists, as they say – and ultimately, when we refuse to give up, we end up struggling to let go.

Syd was a warrior, a fighter, a hero – but I became acutely aware that it all came at a high price. A price I was no longer willing to pay.

HIS FINAL MESSAGE TO ME: 14TH FEBRUARY 2019

*I love you. I'm still awake – just. It's interesting
times all these drugs and time getting closer.
Having a catheter fit today, it's game over.
I just need to accept it and move on.*

BEAUTIFUL TRAUMA

I have to be brutally honest and say that Syd's final hours on this earth were the most terrifying and traumatic of my life. It did not need to be that way, and more of us need to speak up about the unnecessary nature of these undignified deaths. We must stop the relentless suffering of those with terminal illnesses, and we must acknowledge the effect this suffering has on the loved ones left behind. We must have the courage to speak up about these uncomfortable topics to help those feeling alone and desperate to know that they are not alone.

At our core, as human beings, we seek out love and connection; it's how we thrive in life. We are all one. As above, so below. As within, so without. When we are disconnected from life and others, we spiral. We cannot give and receive love and connection openly unless we speak up and tell our stories – no matter how tough. We are, after all, storytellers. Our stories are the glue that holds us together. By sharing them, we begin to realise we are all the same; the challenges we face may be different, but at the crux of it all we experience the same feelings and emotions. Our stories make us stronger and give us hope in what can feel like hopeless situations.

One story I want to share with you from his final day on this earthly plane – and I hang on to this memory for dear life – is something which highlights that even in the most traumatic of moments there is always something beautiful to observe when there is love ever present.

You may recall my story of the way Syd came into this world, in 1983; as my mum described in detail, it was a genuine struggle. Ironically, he left the world in the same way he'd entered it: he was unable to breathe. My mum felt every moment of it with him at both ends of his life. She had sat and slept next to him every single day for six weeks at the hospice. She barely left the room, never mind the hospice – as was evident in the fact that she never wore a pair of shoes the entire time she was there. Her dedication to Syd wasn't something she had to try at – this was natural, indisputable, unconditional love. And as I sat at the end of his bed on that Sunday afternoon, 17th February 2019, after nine hours of what can only be described as painful labour, I watched on as my mum held her baby once again in her arms. I was utterly debilitated, as if frozen in time. The energy in the room was intense. As we all sat in desperation for it all to stop, suddenly the energy shifted. Unbeknown to any of us, my brother Dylan had received a text message from his wife telling him to open a window, in order to help Syd's spirit release. And as he did this, I watched on as my mum rocked her baby back and forth. It felt as though the world had stopped at that moment and we were the only people left on earth. No longer desperate for her baby to stay awake, my mum– searching desperately for a way to help her baby let go– dipped her head, kissed his cheek, and repeatedly whispered, 'Go leepies, go leepies, go leepies.'

And just like that, he went leepies.

I hold on to that memory as one of the single most beautiful moments I have ever witnessed – knowing that Syd was encapsulated in his mother's love as he left this world and returned to his original home. It reminds me of a text message my beautiful childhood friend sent me in the months following his death, in a bid to help me find some comfort. I don't remember them verbatim, but she said something to this effect:

'Do you remember when you were in labour with Louis, and you were in excruciating pain for all those hours, and you wanted to die because it was so painful and so horrible? Do you also remember the utter euphoria, relief, and joy you felt once it was over? Maybe, just maybe, that's what Syd's death was like. Just keep imagining the euphoria he finally felt.'

These were perhaps some of the most helpful words anyone said to me in those first fragile months following his death. It also reminded me of my mum's words of advice before I went into labour with my boys, when she said, 'Just remember, Kay – it's pain, but it's pain with a purpose.'

We must hang on to these words from those we love. Sometimes they can be lifesavers in times of great need.

For me, Syd's death was not the peaceful moment I had been promised. My grief has been defined by those moments, and the post-traumatic stress symptoms I have suffered since will have everlasting effects on my life. I made a promise to my brother that he wouldn't suffer, and the system failed me – it failed us both – in the worst way.

But as I once heard the author Elizabeth Lesser say, 'you can break down, or you can break open', and that's exactly what I did. I broke open.

PART THREE

REMEMBERING

CHAPTER FOURTEEN: GETTING OUT OF MY OWN WAY

You are the only problem you will ever have,
and you are the only solution.
Bob Procter

In the early weeks and months following Syd's death, I was lost, an empty husk of a person. I was sleepwalking from room to room and place to place, searching for something that was no longer there. Everything had lost its meaning. I stopped writing in my journal, unable to string a sentence together. My mind was swirling with thoughts of fear, panic and pain, and no matter how hard I tried, I couldn't find any words in the human language that would accurately express my feelings. So I stopped trying. I couldn't pick up a book. I couldn't speak publicly at his funeral – which was out of character for me. I've often heard people express that they become totally numb after such a loss, and I look back now on those first few weeks in the aftermath of his death and can relate; it was as if I experienced a blackout.

A month or so later, though, I was the complete opposite. I had *all* the feelings. These trapped feelings expressed themselves through several panic attacks, and my anxiety was so heightened that I was unable to work. My grief had overpowered me and hijacked my mind and body, and what I didn't realise then was that I was suffering with post-traumatic stress symptoms. As Syd's life force exited his physical body on that cold Sunday afternoon in February, it seemed as if most of mine went with it. All that was left was a small, distant pilot light. But even in the depths of my personal despair, I knew I just had to hang on and focus on that minute flicker of hope, and trust that one day it would begin to burn brighter.

In January 2019, just one month before Syd died, Rick had an elective abdominal surgical procedure which went drastically wrong. He was supposed to be in and out of hospital within the week and was expected to recover quickly – but instead, in what would prove to be the beginning of another difficult phase of our lives, he contracted sepsis and within one week of his initial operation was taken into emergency surgery to save his life, which left him with a temporary colostomy bag. This was his worst fear realised. He spent a week in the intensive care unit, so every day for two weeks as my brother was dying, I drove 120 miles from hospital bed to hospice bed, alternating the grip of my husband's hand with my brother's hand. As a result, I found myself in a constant unnatural, hypervigilant state for months, which would later contribute to struggles with my mental health.

Most of us know that the 'fight or flight' response is necessary for our survival as a species. The law of nature means that every cell of our being is encoded with highly complex information and instructions which are ready to be launched into action whenever we're faced with any dangerous (or apparently dangerous) situation. This process will more often than not save your life in an acute situation, like if you were about to be hit by a train or being chased by a lion. Those are, of course, extreme situations. But when that response is switched on continuously – in times of chronic stress – we are flooded with cortisol and adrenaline on a permanent basis, eventually leading to degradation of our body and mind.

It is therefore both a blessing and a curse that, as a family, we're extremely good at managing in a crisis situation. We somehow seem to be able to muster all the resources we can find to just keep going, even when everything seems to be against us. We are extremely resilient and strong; however, we don't seem to know how and when to switch it off. Often, subtle physical and mental symptoms begin to show as a result, and the cycle continues. I knew deep down that I had to change the way I managed my stress. As often happens to many of us, though, I was looking in the wrong place. The answer wasn't to stay busy and distracted; it was, in fact, the exact opposite. It was to stop, be present and be still.

THE LOBSTER

Not too long ago, I saw a short video, which you can find on YouTube, by an American rabbi and psychiatrist, Dr Abraham J. Twerski, in which he talks about an article he read in the dentist's waiting room about lobsters and how they grow, and how this relates directly to how we as humans can grow in the face of adversity. It goes a little something like this:

Lobsters are soft animals living within a rigid shell. That rigid shell does not expand. As the lobster grows, that shell becomes very confining and the lobster feels under pressure and uncomfortable, so it goes under a rock to protect itself as it casts off its shell and produces a new one. Eventually, over time, the same thing happens again. The lobster becomes uncomfortable and repeats the process over and over. If the lobster lived in our world, it would go to the doctor and would be prescribed an antidepressant or a Valium. This would stop the discomfort, but the lobster would never get out of its shell.

Just like the lobster, I was deeply uncomfortable and in intense pain. I needed a safe place to take off my shell. Never did I imagine I would find that safe space during a global pandemic.

On 23rd March 2020 the cogs of the thunderous global machine completely and utterly fell off, and the world stopped in the scariest fashion. A worldwide pandemic hit: a mystery virus called coronavirus forced almost every single country across the world to come to a standstill. Although it was frightening initially – our own business, like so many others, had to close immediately, and we had no idea how we would survive – in the chaos of those first few days, I couldn't help but welcome the excuse to stop the madness of the Truman Show. I was struggling with my grief and with my new existence in a world without Syd. I suddenly found myself with time and stillness. Time to hear my own thoughts and breathe a sigh of relief – I could almost feel Mother Nature breathing a sigh of relief with me.

The first lockdown here in the UK was like a surreal dream – or nightmare, depending on how you want to look at it. It was hard to believe that we couldn't go to work, that we were suddenly racked with fear of germs, and we were not allowed to hug anyone outside of our household. I still find it crazy to believe we did all of that. It was an unsettling time in so many ways, and terribly destructive mentally; we are only just experiencing the effects now, and I believe we will feel them for decades to come. Once I accepted what was happening, I turned my focus to using it as an opportunity to turn inwards and do what my true self had been instructing me to do for months. I didn't know it then, but I was about to embark on an intense journey of spiritual and personal growth. I ordered countless books on spirituality, self-mastery, self-discovery; I looked for inspirational podcasts, started to practise yoga every day, and began to make healthier choices in my diet. It was a long road ahead, but I knew that I had to start somewhere. I knew I had all the answers.

One morning, just a few days into lockdown, I was sitting in my living room – it was early, and the sunlight was streaming through a gap in the curtains. As it shone on my feet, I basked in the glory of the rays warming my body from the bottom up. I took my first mouthful of tea of the day, then popped the cup on the side table and picked up my journal. As I put pen to paper, I thought about how empty I felt inside. I looked up at the photo of Syd and me on the bookcase and repeated over and over in my head 'I need you here, I need you here – come back, come back'. Oh, how I wished he could hear me.

As I continued to think about this gaping hole inside me, I suddenly recalled a message I had sent him. I picked up my phone and scrolled back to 5th February 2019. It said:

> *I know you know this, but I have to say I've never felt so heartbroken. I just need you to know that I will never be able to replace the void you are going to leave me with. My life will carry on, I know that, but it won't ever be the same. I've held back saying a lot of this for fear of upsetting you, but I felt the time was right.*

He replied: 'I know. Everything leaves a void.'

'Everything leaves a void' . . . as those words lingered in my mind, I pondered for a moment, and it suddenly dawned on me. It isn't the person or thing that you lose that leaves the void; the void is always there inside of you. I had been using people and things outside of myself to fill a void when truly I needed to fill it myself. And I had been doing this for decades. I was the answer to all of my problems. I needed to become whole. On my own.

THE LION

Courage doesn't happen when you have all the answers. It happens when you are ready to face the questions you have been avoiding your whole life.
Shannon L. Alder

In order to continue my journey along the yellow brick road, just like the Lion in *The Wizard of Oz*, I had to be brave once again – I had to dig deeper than I had ever dug before and find my courage. And this time I was ready. I had nothing to lose. I knew that nothing would ever be as bad as watching my brother die – and in a desperate bid to avoid my brother's fate, I began to question everything about my life. Not just skimming the edges, as I had done in the past, or trying to make messy things look neat and tidy. No – this time I got uncomfortably honest with myself and those around me. I needed to understand what was holding me back from feeling the happiness and peace I knew, deep down, that I deserved in my life. How had I become so reliant on others to make me happy? Where was this elusive happiness?

As I inhaled book after book and journaled so hard I couldn't write any more, one thing became glaringly obvious. I was a co-dependent. *What, me? Little Miss Independent? Surely not!* Let me tell you, it's very confronting to face yourself in a way you've never had the courage to face yourself before. It was like my life flashed before me as I saw all the decisions I'd made, all the victimhood I'd adopted, the story I'd told myself, and all the unhappiness I had created throughout my adult life. I had done that. The truth was, all of my happiness in life was based on whether the people around me were happy or not. I only felt safe if everyone else was safe.

I recently read a wonderful little paragraph on Instagram (author unknown) which for me perfectly demonstrated my need to be loved and where it may have come from. It said:

'A lot of us have habits we learnt as kids to feel safe, like:

- Helping
- Being perfect, positive, upbeat
- Not needing support from others
- Being strong, independent
- Staying out of the way

And we can never stop because we are still afraid that it's those things that we do that make love not go away.'

As I delved deeper, things started to make sense. I discovered I was what is known as a highly sensitive person, and realised my sensitive soul, buried inside that little girl's body all those years ago, was desperate to be loved, to be seen, to be heard. I had this deep need to be validated; I feared being abandoned, ignored, and left alone. So I would do anything to keep those around me close – even if it suffocated them.

As more revelations bubbled to the surface and as my post-traumatic symptoms following Syd's death continued to cause havoc in my everyday life, I decided it was time to seek some professional help once again. I knew I needed some sort of guidance, someone to help me make sense of everything.

I couldn't do this on my own. I was scared and unnerved by the sinking sand I was wading through every day. It was impacting my work, my marriage, and my relationship with myself. I felt like I was losing a grip on who I was.

Now, therapy isn't for everyone– this I know. It may not be your thing; it may not even be accessible for you, something I am aware needs to change. But my personal experience with counsellors and therapists has been incredibly helpful. Family support is incredible for those who are lucky enough to have it – and I do– but I needed someone outside who could observe my life without judgement and without any preconceived views. Someone who wasn't so close to all the emotional baggage I lugged around with me. I also needed a safe place to share my deepest hurts and to find a way to start to make sense of my new life – a life without my brother. His death had shaken my life up, unearthing parts of me that I didn't even know were there or which were long since forgotten. It prompted me to question everything about my life and discover whether it was in fact what I really wanted. One thing I knew: I did not want to live with any regrets. Syd had reminded me of this when he sent me a message in January 2019, just one month before his death:

I've realised I'm annoyed because I've just realised how I should have lived my life, how I want to live my life, and now it's too late and I'm not lucky enough to have a second chance. Bummer.

I promised myself that in order to honour his life, I would grab this second chance at life that he didn't get; I would make sure I lived in alignment with who I truly was, not what everyone else expected of me. I had always known that I was connected to Syd forever through a love that would transcend lifetimes and physical places, so we could still do it together. I could take him with me – in my heart. He could still be part of my story; he had just transformed from the physical being he had appeared to be on this earth into the pure spiritual being he had always been.

A SURPRISING SPEECH

The timing was awful. It was February 2019, and I had started a new job – back with the same company I had worked for in South Australia, but this time their UK head office, although I worked mostly from home. It was meant to be one of the most exciting times of my life, but here I was, in my brother's final weeks, leaving the hospice to travel hundreds of miles to attend an annual sales conference in Brighton. To ease my conscience, I had discussed my imminent departure with the consultant and my beautiful friend Katie. She was a complementary therapist who had been supporting my family during our time at the hospice, but she also happened to be an old friend from school. We hadn't seen each other in over twenty-five years, but by some incredible stroke of luck, we had been reunited – albeit under tragic circumstances. It was so comforting to me to have someone who had been such a dear friend here in this moment that I could trust whole-heartedly with my and my family's wishes.

'Really, how long do you think he's got? I mean, I know you can't be certain, but you must have some idea – you've must've seen this so many times,' I said as we stood in the corridor outside Syd's room. We were talking in hushed voices, trying to avoid even one word being picked up by those bat ears. It wasn't that I was trying to hide the facts of his date with death – he was well aware of his upcoming appointment – but I was trying to hide my guilt for trying to escape.

'I really couldn't say,' Katie replied. Her eyes softened as she looked at me sympathetically. She knew my pain, having lost her own father to cancer four years earlier. She held my hands and said, 'I think you'll be fine – I don't think you will miss it. He's certainly not giving us any signs yet that it's hours away.'

'OK,' I thought, 'I can do this.' I would be there and back in just a matter of days, and I could keep in constant contact with my brother on WhatsApp; I told myself that if I needed to, I could jump on a train and be back within hours, even if he started to deteriorate. So, with my guilt numbed, I said my goodbyes and headed home to pack my bags.

As I sat on the train, swigging back my mini bottles of Prosecco to anaesthetise the pain, I laughed along with my colleagues, trying to find some sort of relief in the distraction. WhatsApp messages continued to pop up from Syd, alerting me to everything that was happening back at the hospice. My heart would lurch every time the screen lit up, as the horrendous guilt for leaving him reared up once again, but I quickly pushed it down, knowing that I was now in self-preservation mode – or even in denial.

By this time I had worked in the corporate world for over twenty years, and I had attended annual sales conferences every year for over ten of those years. I knew exactly what to expect: strategy meetings, awards ceremonies, fancy dinners, and a lot of excessive drinking. It seemed so far removed from what was actually going on in my *real* life back at home.

One agenda item I looked forward to every year was the motivational speaker. I loved being inspired by others; I was forever captivated when listening to stories of how other human beings overcame adversity. This year wasn't any different. As I walked across the main ballroom, heading for a large round table at the centre of the room, I couldn't help but feel uplifted by Rag'n'Bone Man's hit song 'Giant' booming through the huge speakers surrounding me. As the goosebumps created by the music and the energy in the room started to subside, I felt energised and excited to finally hear our guest speaker. Now, for the life of me I cannot remember his name, but what I do remember is that he was a South African rugby player, probably in his thirties, with dark hair and a strong presence. As we all put our hands together to welcome him to the stage, I won't deny that I did an internal eye roll and thought, 'Here we go – another sports team analogy of how we are going to compete and win at all costs, regardless of how many people we have to walk over to hold the winner's trophy.' But what I heard was something quite different, and it was a message that would change my life.

His entire talk was centred around his coach and his unique ability to completely change the culture of a team and bring about huge success. And what surprised me the most was that the focus wasn't on how physically fit they were, or how strategically the game was played (although of course this was important) – it was the happiness and contentedness of his team, both as individuals and as a group. His belief was that when a player is fulfilled and happy in all aspects of their life, this will be reflected in their ability to play at the highest level of sport and achieve success. He summed this up by sharing with his team the three essentials for happiness that he swore by.

Now, at this point, I was absolutely transfixed. I mean, this man was speaking my language – and who doesn't want to know the key to lifelong happiness?

I watched in anticipation as the three essentials to happiness appeared on the big screen. I need to point out here that these essentials weren't made up by the coach; they have been quoted by several people in the past, most commonly Alexander Chalmers, a Scottish writer. But I was only hearing them for the first time, and it wasn't important to me who wrote them. What was important was the profound effect they had on me that day.

Three essentials to happiness:

1. Something to do
2. Someone to love
3. Something to hope for

As I repeated these three statements over and over in my mind, I started to wonder whether it even *was* happiness that I had been in search of, or whether it was something much deeper. I started to believe that what I was actually searching for was inner peace.

As the pandemic marched on into 2020, just thirteen months later, I would recall these three statements, and they would become the foundation for my survival – a scaffold, if you like, upon which I could rebuild my life.

CHAPTER FIFTEEN: BACK TO NATURE

You are a miracle. Every cell and atom in your body is divine and alive, intricate, sophisticated, efficient, and perfect. Lack, illness, and discord aren't par for the course, they're not the goals of any of us. They're simply the byproducts of limited, fearful and under-par thinking.

Mike Dooley

When I was upset as a child, like most children, I wanted to escape. Sometimes it would be expressed in the form of a mental escape into my diaries, where I found some relief, but at other times I would physically escape to a small woodland about two hundred yards from our house. I would pack my green and purple rucksack with what were then my essentials for life: a couple of broken biscuits, a drink, one of my beloved books, my diary, a pen, and a pair of pyjamas (which never got used). Memories of these escapes are still vivid. They usually consisted of the same pattern of events. I would feel upset, overwhelmed with emotion, and plan my escape early in the day. Later on, in the afternoon, I would gingerly open my bedroom window and shimmy down the ladders from my brother's wooden cabin bed out onto the ground outside. I would marvel at my own sneakiness at getting away without my parents or my brothers even noticing – finally free! Just like Dick Whittington before he embarked on his travels to London, I would swing my rucksack over my shoulder and onto my back and make my way up past the village green, arriving just a few minutes later at my destination – my own little paradise. I hated the world and everyone in it during those moments of escape; life wasn't fair, and as far as I was concerned, *no one* understood me. I was determined that I was never going to return to that 'stupid house'.

I would clamber my way through the densely wooded area, stamping down on the crisp foliage, ensuring a way out when I needed it. Like most children, it was my worst nightmare to get lost. I still recall the day we lost Syd in the middle of Bradford city centre when he was about five years old; the sheer terror on my mum's face is still etched into my memory. Once I had a clearly marked path, I would begin to relax and find myself awash with peace at the thought of my next few hours of solitude – away from those 'stupid people'.

Although I had obvious reasons for my escape to my tranquil spot, as a young child there was something unexplainable about why it made me feel the way I did on the inside. I didn't have the language for it then, but as part of my HSP trait I needed an environment where I could process the world around me in a deep and reflective way, without overstimulation. This is partly why being in nature on my own allowed my heightened emotions to subside. Nature had called me, and I unknowingly responded. The comforting sight of the lush green oak trees, the sweet sounds of the birds, and the warm, earthy smell of Mother Nature wrapped around all my senses, instantly healing and soothing my upset. These were moments, I now know, of being brought back to myself; I was recalibrating my nervous system without even consciously being aware of it.

To me, that's the beauty of nature. It all just happens if you just let it be. Like when we breathe – although we can breathe consciously (one of the few functions of the body that can be controlled consciously), we more often than not are unaware of our breathing. Our chest will continue to rise and fall from the moment we are born until the moment we die. Nor do we have to work hard to digest the food we eat, pump our own heart, or grow our own hair and fingernails. It all just happens, as if by magic – isn't it incredible? From womb to tomb, this is happening without any of our involvement at all, each and every single moment of every day. How is this possible? The law of nature is how.

'Nature' has become my word for God. For me it represents an intelligence that is bigger than us, an intelligence that doesn't need our interference – only our cooperation with it. And the more aligned to nature we can be, the more access we will have to the healing powers of this divine intelligence. But we just can't help ourselves, can we? Somewhere along the way, we got it all wrong and we truly came to believe that we're superior to every living thing in the universe, and we now find ourselves experiencing the painful result of that arrogance. What we are seeing is an imbalance in nature; the earth is malfunctioning, and as a species we have become so imbalanced that disease is now rife throughout our global populations. I don't think anyone would disagree with this observation.

Nature recognises nature; it tends to malfunction when anything tries to 'fake it'. The saying 'you are what you eat' is not some cliché or play on words; it has real meaning. If we eat junk, we feel like junk. If we don't move, we stagnate. If we close our heart energy off and are unable to express love, we live our life in fear and consequently get sick. Sadly, many of us have become completely disconnected from nature, which in turn leaves us disconnected from ourselves. I would call on this knowledge from my childhood visits to that small piece of woodland just yards from my home as I would begin to remember my place in nature over thirty years later.

LESS IS MORE

Once I had accepted that the void in me that Syd had left behind had in fact been there all along, I set about finding ways to fill the void and bring myself back to wholeness, as nature intended. 'But where to start?' I wondered.

It can be so overwhelming when we're constantly told by others what we should or should not be doing. Usually this unsolicited advice comes from a good place – and goodness knows I have needed advice at times – but at the end of the day, what we really need is to be listened to and be allowed the space to work out what is best for ourselves. The only person who knew what was best for me was *me*. And I needed to start listening to that little girl in the woodland again. I kept turning inward and tried to ignore the noise around me, including the good-willed advice of others. I decided to eliminate all goal-setting practices, throw the five-year plans out of the window, and instead start a list of my values – what was important to me at my core – and how practising these values could lead to a greater sense of wholeness. It had to be my truth, no one else's. I knew instinctively that I needed to direct my energy towards the things that mattered to me, and that in order for any of this to become achievable or realistic, I would need to keep it simple.

I began to journal a list of value-based 'soul instructions'. And every time I wrote a list, I would later refine it. I found that by writing these lists over and over, I was able to eliminate what was no longer important. I found it so difficult at first to shake off my old habits of sticking with the list – but over time, I came to understand that it's OK to change my mind if something is no longer working for me. How I see it now is that it's just like trying on different pairs of shoes until we find a pair that fits. It would make for a painful existence to walk around in ill-fitting shoes every day, now, wouldn't it?

SICK TO MY STOMACH

It was the early morning of 23rd March 2019. As I waited in my dressing gown for the kettle to boil, I stood in the quiet semi-darkness of my living room and conducted what had turned into my morning ritual of gazing across at the photo of me and Syd on the mantlepiece. I was pining for his return. It still didn't feel real that he had gone. As I glanced at the box his ashes were in, a pang of grief swelled up in my stomach and tears began to stream down my face. I closed my eyes and prayed that I would hear his voice; I needed his guidance. I just needed something, anything that might help me take a step forward into some sort of life without him. Then I heard him. 'Go to yoga, do you hear me? Remember how much I said I wanted to go, and I never did? Well now I can't – but you can. It will help you. Go.'

Was this his voice – or was it mine? The two crossed over in so many ways. Regardless, I felt compelled to follow the message. I booked in that same evening for a yoga class just five hundred yards up the road.

As I laid my mat down along with ten other soul searchers, I felt sure I wouldn't last the whole session – but I was here now, and what did I have to lose? I tried to empty my mind, and as I took some deep breaths, carefully following the instructions from Ms S, our yoga teacher, I settled in. I have to admit that despite all the alternative healing work I had embraced up to then, there was still that sceptical part of me saying, 'What can yoga really do for me? I mean, it's just stretching and breathing, isn't it?' But during this session, something happened that changed my opinion completely.

I found the rhythmic motion of the transition between poses calming, and it gave my mind focus. I loved following someone else's lead, particularly as I didn't seem to be able to make any decisions for myself since grief had taken over.

As we reached the end of the hour-long session, we were all relieved to lie flat on our backs in what is known as *Savasana* (corpse pose). This is usually a serene moment of quiet at the end of the session which everyone looks forward to. As Ms S began to guide us through a short meditation, I suddenly felt an overwhelming surge of emotion. It came from my toes all the way up to the top of my head. As my eyes filled with tears, I didn't seem to be able to prevent the cascade of emotions spilling quietly from my eyes to my ears and onto my yoga mat. Then, as if from nowhere, an intense nausea rushed over me, and a cramping in my stomach suddenly made itself known. I felt for sure that I would need to scream out any second. As I gripped onto the sides of my yoga mat, I let out an internal scream instead, just hoping I could hang on until the end of the session and sneak out without causing any fuss or commotion.

My egoic mind couldn't understand what was occurring and was insistent on telling me that I would surely embarrass myself among these ten other strangers, or that I would die an agonising death from what must be an internal bleed. Luckily, my spirit was telling me that what was happening was in fact a significant emotional and spiritual shift brought on by the physical movements of the yoga asanas. My body was forcing an emotional release of feelings that had been buried in the cells of my being. It was painful and scary, but absolutely necessary for some sort of healing to take place.

As I stood up slowly, I felt like I'd been hit by a truck. My head felt thick and fuzzy, my tummy was still aching, and in all honesty, I wasn't sure I ever wanted to practise yoga again. I rolled up my mat, trying not to let on what had happened, and put it away neatly in the cupboard. I quietly whispered my thanks to Ms S, and left.

But despite the experience being strange and unpleasant, I just knew I had to go back. I had a strong sense it was going to play a significant role in my healing, and it became one of the most profound physical aspects of my 'something to do'.

THE FEATHER

It was a Sunday afternoon – 31st May 2020, smack bang in the middle of the first COVID-19 lockdown in the UK. Like most families, we were at home trying to balance the negative feelings of isolation from our family, friends, so-called normal life, the devastation of our failing business, and the utter joy of this unexpected time at home during one of the warmest, driest summers on record. I was sitting at the table outside, baking in the early summer sun, reading, and battling a hangover from the night before. As I mentioned in Chapter One, I started drinking alcohol when I was just thirteen years old, and despite spending the eight years prior to 2020 researching everything I could find relating to cancer prevention, how to heal the body from chronic dis-eases, the mind–body connection, self-mastery, and how to live my life closer to nature, I still insisted on ignoring my unhealthy relationship with this socially accepted drug.

Alcohol, I have learnt, is a tricky subject for most of us,

mainly due to the fact that for the most part it's not only socially acceptable in our culture, but often expected and encouraged. We can even find ourselves outcast from the group if we don't consume it, which leads most of us to spend our entire lives never questioning our feelings about it – or worse still, never recognising when the balance has tipped too far in alcohol's favour and our very lives are at risk.

Well, on this particular day, something happened which prompted one of the biggest lifestyle changes I had ever undertaken.

I had been a regular drinker all of my adult life – I used alcohol to celebrate, commiserate, tolerate, and medicate – but since Syd's death, my drinking habits had become worse. It doesn't really matter what or how much I was drinking; what matters is that I was becoming aware of the damage it was causing to my mind, body and soul, and that my reasons for drinking had become worrisome to me. I had always known deep down that it wasn't good for me, but the desire to fit in and the fear of missing out were so strong that I just carried on regardless. Unlike me, Syd had never really been much of a drinker and couldn't understand why I drank the way I did; he never judged me, but for years I had his niggling voice in my head telling me to take a break from it. I hadn't taken a break since 2010, when I took three weeks off during a failed 'dry January'.

As I struggled through my third or fourth hair of the dog that Sunday afternoon in the sunshine, I suddenly felt that familiar anxiety rising and decided to get inside, out of the fierce afternoon sun, and rest on the sofa. As soon as my head hit the cushions, I could hear my heartbeat racing and thumping in my chest. This immediately activated the fear signals in my brain.

'Rick!' I yelled, hoping he would hear my voice.

He came rushing down the stairs. 'What's wrong? What's happening?' He didn't wait too long to hear my response, and before I knew what was going on, an ambulance was called.

When they arrived, they performed an ECG, and I was taken to the local hospital, where they planned to do further tests. As I sat in the corridor, nervously waiting for a bed, I was convinced I was having a heart attack; although I had experienced panic attacks in the past, my brain was still telling me I was about to die. For those of you reading this who have experienced a panic attack, you will understand what I mean, and know just how real and scary it is.

I'd arrived in A&E around teatime, with the paramedics assuring me that although my resting heart rate was one hundred beats per minute, they were confident this wasn't a heart attack– but I was to wait for the test results to confirm it for sure. My inner voice was whispering to me and letting me know what the problem was: I was drinking too much, and in order to improve my physical health, I needed to remove alcohol from my life for an extended period of time. This inner knowing just wasn't enough, though; I needed a sign from Syd. I sat in the hospital corridor, mask-adorned, socially distanced, and feeling sorry for myself. As I pondered how I would even begin to make the changes I needed to make, a nurse walked towards me and said, 'If you'd like to come with me, Kay, we have a bed ready just over here, where the doctor will come and see you.'

'Thank you so much,' I replied quietly from behind my mask.

As she motioned towards the empty bed in the corner near the window, I thought about all the times Syd must have been ushered towards an array of hospital beds, and the feelings of fear that must have conjured up for him. Just as I approached the bed, with Syd at the forefront of my mind, there it was: my sign. Right in the centre of the bed, on the clean, crisp sheets, lay a single grey and white feather. I couldn't believe my eyes. Finding a feather isn't such an unusual thing in and of itself, but the circumstances on that day were amazing to me. I mean, how on earth – in this sterile ward just off the main A&E department at the Royal Lancaster Infirmary, with no ability for windows to be opened – had a bird's feather found itself nestled on the freshly laundered white linen? And not only that; out of all the beds in the hospital, it had found its way to mine. I carefully picked it up and hopped onto the bed, and as I sat there, my mouth still agape at what had just happened, I looked up and saw the doctor approaching.

'Nice to meet you, Mrs Backhouse. My name is Dr So. We have received your test results, and I am pleased to say you are not having a heart attack.'

Instant relief ensued.

She continued, 'I do have a question for you, though.

Do you drink alcohol at all?'

How was she doing this? Was she reading my mind?

Unlike every other time I had been asked about my drinking habits by a doctor, I decided to tell the truth. Without hesitation, I replied, 'Yes. Yes, I do. I drink too much, and I know I do. It's really strange you should ask, as it's something I've been thinking about stopping lately.'

'It seems perhaps now might be the right time,' she said with a reassuring smile.

I was discharged from the hospital that evening, and didn't pick up a drink for the next seventy-one days.

CHAPTER SIXTEEN:
LETTING GO

*What happens if we let go, if we stop trying to
keep the world orbiting and just let it whirl? It'll
keep right on whirling. It'll stay right on track
with no help from us. And we'll be free and
relaxed enough to enjoy our place on it.*
Melody Beattie

As I write these words, it's approaching 7.30 a.m. on a freezing cold Sunday morning in January. I part the window shutters and look out over the rolling hills of the Lake District, and my gaze fixes on the mist of the morning rising in fragmented wisps into the cool air. I take a deep and grateful breath for the gentle dawn of a new day and turn to face an empty bed. I decide it's time to stop procrastinating and get back to writing.

I grab my laptop and jump back into bed, snuggling under the covers with a cup of tea, all the while trying to ignore the negative self-talk swirling in my head. *You could've written a whole chapter by now. Are you even committed? What happened to all the plans you made? You're never going to get this book finished. Then what will everyone think?*

You see, I'm not even at home, so I don't have the excuse of distractions. I came away on a four-day yoga retreat.

As a retreat virgin, I didn't know exactly what to expect, other than a few downward dogs and hours of writing. My intentions were to lock myself away and finish my book, just like they do in the movies. But, as John Lennon (among others) said, life is what happens to us while we're making other plans, so instead I've spent the first two days practising yoga, crying my way through healing ceremonies, reading, walking, talking to like-minded soul searchers, meditating, and embracing the beautiful surroundings of this seventeenth-century stone-built Cumbrian farm, hosted by the calm and graceful shamanic goddess that is Stephanie. Surely there's nothing wrong with that – right? Well, of course not, to an outsider looking in, but for me – the recovering perfectionist – it has become another lesson in how to let go of those perfectly made plans, hand them over to the universe and have faith that it's OK to let life happen and unfold as it should. I tell myself repeatedly to just *be*, instead of trying to *do* all the time. It makes me wonder how often we stop the natural flow of life. How often do we try to control what is happening around us, attempting to mould our days into our neatly planned diaries and to-do lists? I came here with my set intentions for 2023 and my neat list of 'things to do' and once again it all changed. Quite apt, really, that I should be beginning this chapter on letting go as I continue to practise what has become my greatest lesson in life: how to let go. But what is it, exactly, that we are trying to let go of?

BOX OF FROGS

Throughout my journey of learning to let go, I've come across many great teachers, authors and sages, both past and present, who have shared their wisdom on the subject. One of my favourites by a mile is Michael Singer, the spiritual teacher and author of *The Untethered Soul*. He has a wonderfully simple way of describing the emotional baggage we often carry around with us throughout life, and how it can block our flow state if we don't learn to process this stuff and let it go. He refers to our natural state as a running river flowing through life; over time, we collect an enormous amount of emotional baggage, and if not dealt with, these emotions appear as 'rocks in the river' and disturb the flow. Yes, the water can move around these disturbances, but the more rocks that appear, the more they disrupt the flow, eventually blocking the river.

So what are these disturbances? I've come to know that they are, more often than not, one or a variety of the following: anger, envy, grief, rage, frustration, resentment, sadness, and bitterness. These are all the things we claim we don't like and want to let go of, but somehow we do the complete opposite and hang on to them for dear life. I have come to believe that what lies beneath all these disturbances is fear – fear of a life without the stories we've told ourselves, the belief systems passed down through generations; fear that without them we won't know how to be in the world, and we'll lose our foothold, our place in the world. So we stay afraid, in a perpetual cycle of discomfort, just because it's all we have ever known.

Throughout my life, I have often heard the phrase 'mad as a box of frogs'. I always thought it was a funny term to describe someone who was so-called crazy – yet now, just like Mr Singer's rocks in the water, I think it perfectly describes the disturbances that we accumulate in this lifetime. If we don't learn to let go of our frogs, we can drive ourselves crazy.

Imagine for a moment that you start your life with an empty box. Throughout adolescence and into adulthood, you accumulate a number of frogs in your box. These frogs – fears – come to you in a number of ways. Often, other people will put the frogs in your box – sometimes they will take frogs from their own box and put them in yours – but the hardest of all to spot are the ones that we put in there ourselves. The frogs you accumulate might include the boyfriend who cheated on you, the brother who repeatedly teased you, the friend who gossiped about you behind your back, the business partner who stole from you, the parent who neglected you, the guilt you felt about a lie you told, or the shame you carry from the dreadful decision you made. These are all things that can and do happen to all of us in life, and they can trigger emotions that cause us to act out of character – becoming mad as a box of frogs – if they are not addressed.

So how do we address them, and what happens if we don't?

When we hang on tightly to our box of frogs, not only does it become too heavy and unmanageable to carry, but it also prevents us from making room to hold anything else – like all of the love, joy, happiness, bliss, gratitude, and peace that is our birthright. We become closed off with fear, and opportunities for embracing love are often missed. We are so distracted by managing our box of frogs that we can't see there's a simple way of placing the box down and setting ourselves free. Awareness of the box isn't enough, as when we become aware our initial reaction is often to throw the box directly in the face of the person we believe has caused the disturbance – this is called 'projection' – and I can tell you from first-hand experience that this is not an effective way of dealing with your frogs.

In 2007, right before we moved to Australia, I decided to throw my box of frogs at my mum. Over the years, my collection of frogs had become lively. They were hopping up and down, backward and forward, and I was desperate to rid myself of these pesky creatures. So I decided to write my mum a letter. In it I would detail all the reasons why I was so unhappy with my life, and link all of that unhappiness to my mum. Of course, this wasn't true. It was just that I had accumulated so many frogs during my teens and twenties, without addressing a single one, that I had become confused and extremely uncomfortable trying to carry them around with me. Now, that's not to say that the things I said in that letter were all untrue – there were definitely past hurts in there that needed to be addressed – but it was the fact that I had kept these frogs all to myself. Instead of carefully lifting the frogs out one by one and facing them before gently releasing them into the wild, I launched a hit and run attack right before I left the country. Needless to say, this wasn't my finest moment.

FORGIVENESS

There's a saying, 'It's not the snake bite that kills you, it's the venom'.

And I genuinely believe that we must forgive those who have hurt us (including ourselves), otherwise we are the only one who suffers.

Ever since I was a little girl, I've always been a forgiving person. I don't tend to hold grudges – often because I don't like conflict – and my empathic, sensitive nature means I understand other people's pain and suffering and will more often than not look for the reasons behind why someone may act in a less than favourable manner, rather than wanting to lynch them. *Oh, they must have had a difficult childhood. They must be unhappy with their own life.* This attitude towards others, although celebrated, has often left me open to being mocked. I have been called 'gullible', 'too soft', 'weak' . . . and there's no doubt that in some cases, they were right. I have had to learn to be more assertive in order to avoid others taking advantage of my kind and caring nature, which is of course easier said than done.

Despite my amenable nature, though, I am not immune to my own shadow self – my own deep-rooted disturbances – and have had to do battle with one disturbance in particular which almost ruined my marriage: resentment. Being a co-dependent, this disturbance often comes with the territory. As I have said before, I'm a recovering people-pleaser, and this tends to go hand in hand with a lack of boundaries: never knowing when to say no, always helping others before I would help myself. When Rick and I met, I was young, inexperienced at life and completely unaware of my emotional programming. I didn't know it then, but I was subconsciously seeking approval and validation (by being the good girl) in order to feel safe, accepted, and loved. To achieve this lofty status would mean going along with whatever decisions were made about our lives together – whether I agreed with them or not. Making decisions that did not align with my soul but caused the least amount of friction was my go-to stance in life. I was always desperate to steady the ship and keep things on an even keel and in control – which naturally became suffocating for Rick.

Why did I do this? Well, on reflection I've come to know that most of it was happening on a subconscious level, but it was inextricably linked to the love I had found with Rick, which was real, genuine, magnetic and something I had never felt before. I didn't want to lose it. I couldn't risk being unplugged, cut off, abandoned. I believed I was half a person without him. If I just kept saying yes to every request, then that would keep him happy, and in turn would ensure I felt safe. I came to associate all my people-pleasing with lifting Rick's low mood when he was down or unhappy with life. I wanted to ensure he felt loved and cared for, and ultimately I was trying to avoid my biggest fear – failure. But when we have no boundaries, do not speak up and at the same time attempt to control our situation in ways that make others feel fenced in, then I've come to know that resentment builds on both sides – usually covertly – until one day, bang! Your collective boxes of frogs are spewing all over the place. As I described earlier in the book, grief, anger and resentment are often intertwined with one another. My lack of boundaries and my need to control everything had landed me in an uncomfortable place. I suddenly became aware that I had enabled behaviours in both Rick and myself that weren't healthy and in some cases were downright toxic. It was the reason our relationship would often become stuck.

It has taken me years to work through and unpack my box of frogs, and it's not over yet. I am a work in progress, just like everyone else, and I'm finally OK with that. It can be an ugly process at times, and it requires a level of courage and forgiveness from both sides to make it work. I've found that you have to be willing to make significant changes and allow each other the freedom to express your true feelings without judgement. You have to be willing and open to be in the trenches together and have faith that it is all part of your growth in this life and that you're in it for the long haul. As a friend of mine recently said, 'You have to be willing to adjust and live together in a way that may seem unconventional to others but makes sense to you.' I have also come to believe that the most important relationships in our lives – and particularly our relationship with our life partner – are the ones that offer us the greatest opportunity for growth.

Despite my beliefs as a child, I now know there's no such thing as a perfect marriage – or a perfect life, for that matter; we're all on a journey to remember who we are, what we are capable of, and how we can contribute to this life. That process can be messy, and if you're truly willing to do the work, the mess is unavoidable. The question we must ask ourselves, then, is who we choose to have by our side through the mess, because we're going to have to wade through it regardless. Having processed many of my past resentments, I'm no longer a co-dependent; I don't need Rick to validate me in order for me to feel safe and loved, and I'm no longer desperate for him or anyone else to fix my mess. Now, as the truest version of myself, I choose Rick to be by my side while I figure out my own mess and he figures out his. We are no longer holding each other hostage. What I truly believe has kept us together, despite all the ups and downs and serious hurt we have caused each other, is that we've been willing to have the difficult conversations without judgement and we've never wavered far from the eye of the storm – the calm, peaceful place we both recognise when we look at one another and see that we are both the same. We are human, and we are just trying our best. He has become one of my greatest teachers. As Queen B (Beyoncé) says, your torturer can become your remedy.

As I type this, I am reminded of Don Miguel Ruiz's *Four Agreements* once again:

- Don't make assumptions.
- Don't take things personally.
- Be impeccable with your word.
- Always do your best.

I have found these to be helpful reminders when trying to navigate my way through relationship challenges.

THE GREAT MYSTERY

If you realise that all things change, there is nothing you will try to hold on to. If you weren't afraid of dying, there is nothing you can't achieve. Trying to control the future is like trying to take the master carpenter's place. When you handle the master carpenter's tools, chances are that you'll cut your hand.
Stephen Mitchell, *Tao Te Ching*

Those words are taken from the ancient text of the *Tao Te Ching*, written over 2,500 years ago. These teachings, often known as *The Great Way*, are brimming with Eastern wisdom and knowledge; they quite simply give guidance on how to live a peaceful and contented life by letting go and living in balance with the laws of nature.

I was first drawn to Eastern religions and philosophies back in 2011, just a few months after Syd's initial diagnosis. I was searching for something to steady my resolve. I had lost my faith in anything following my adolescent disillusionment with Western religions, so I was effectively 'winging it' at life, which seems manageable until life throws you a curveball and the suffering seeps in. I suddenly became aware of a hunger for something bigger than me to step in and take over, something or someone to guide me through the enormity of what we were facing as a family. So, right before we were due to set off on a family holiday, I listened to that inner knowing, and it led me unexpectedly straight to the local library. I hadn't set foot in a public library since I attended school over fifteen years earlier, yet here I was standing in the middle aisle, wondering how I got here. As I stood facing the endless rows of books, I seemed to glide instinctively to the section labelled 'Religion and Spirituality'. As I ran my fingers down the spines of these ancient texts, I could sense there was something here just for me. I placed my index finger on a thick, almost intimidating, book and tipped it gently towards me. *Buddhism* was the title; I don't remember the author. All I remember is that I knew this book was for me. I had no idea why, but something told me it was going to help alleviate the pain I felt during this period of my life and would unravel the ghastly knot which seemed to have taken up residence in the centre of my chest for the foreseeable future.

As I looked across the bay, the tide was so far out that I had to squint to see Rick and the boys. They had ventured out enthusiastically with their fishing rods, buckets and nets, all set for a day of sea fishing, likely to return with nothing, but of course the excitement was always in the anticipation.

They would be gone for hours, which meant I could relax, guilt-free, knowing they were enjoying themselves without any input from me. I hurried to my suitcase, which was sitting at the bottom of the bed, and retrieved the book I'd borrowed from the library. As I hoisted the heavy textbook out from underneath my shorts and bikinis, I couldn't help but notice a wave of excitement and curiosity run up and down my body. With the book in one hand and my bottle of beer in the other, I set about getting comfy on the wooden deckchair overlooking the ocean.

There's something so magical, isn't there, about being close to the ocean? It's a place we often think of when we're asked to take our minds somewhere else. Why is that? I don't think it's a coincidence that we all experience this feeling; we are, after all, over seventy per cent water ourselves, and I became convinced during my twenties that being close to the ocean induced a feeling directly related to our oneness with nature. Another example of 'as above, so below'. We have known for centuries that the ocean has a great number of healing effects on our bodies, minds, and spirits. However, this knowledge didn't become popularised in the UK until the mid-eighteenth century when high society needed cures for all kinds of ailments that were rife prior to the Industrial Revolution. It became well known that the seaside offered a number of healing benefits which could be accessed through several modalities: swimming in the salty water (swirling with rich, natural minerals), exposing our bodies to the cold water (cold immersion, which we now know can assist with regulating blood pressure, improving mood, boosting the immune system, and even healing trauma –Wim Hof's work on this is a useful resource for more information), and the simple method of breathing in the positive and negative ions of the sea air. It quickly became known as Mother Nature's pharmacy. I was always happy and at peace with myself and the world around me when sitting by the ocean, and this day was no exception.

As I opened the pages and began reading, something about the story of the Siddhartha Gautama – the Buddha – captured my attention immediately. I could sense a subtle shift inside of me. I was not only captivated by the rich history of this beautiful religion but also hooked by the concept of finding peace within the suffering of life. I mean, how was this even possible? Didn't that go against everything I had been taught? Looking back, I can see that this was the start of my journey back to myself. That book saved me in those months following Syd's diagnosis. I finally had something I could hang on to – something I could truly believe in – and for once it felt like it was my own. No one had instructed me to follow a particular path – it wasn't forced upon me – and not only that, but I also finally felt free to choose aspects of a religion and mould it into what could become my own beliefs about spirituality and the divine. We far too often fall into the trap of believing that we have to run away to live a monastic life on a mountaintop, chanting, for the rest of our time on earth, to finally be at peace, but this just isn't the case. I believe that it's possible to find that peace right where you are.

A couple of years later, I was afforded the opportunity once again to brush up against the wise teachings of the Buddha – this time in Thailand, when I was blessed to visit the Big Buddha in Phuket. We were holidaying with friends, but it hadn't started out well. It was only a few months after my herniated disc and Syd's terminal diagnosis, and we were all in need of some quality family time and a little escape from all the negativity. Within the first day or two, I came down with a horrible sickness bug, which we later found out was running rampant throughout the hotel, with some guests hospitalised and on a drip. What made things worse was how it slowly took down each member of our group, so that getting together on the same day was becoming next to impossible. But on this particular day we finally had some relief, and set about trying to salvage what was left of our holiday. We took a trip together to view the mighty Buddha. Sitting atop Nakkerd Hill, overlooking the Andaman Sea, this sacred statue can be viewed from miles around. On this particular day, not dissimilar to the rest of our time in Thailand, the clouds were heavy, the air was thick, and the humidity was so high that donning the customary scarves to cover my bare skin before ascending the ninety-four steps snaking their way up to the statue didn't fill my dehydrated body with joy. However, nothing was going to spoil the excitement I felt about the experience that awaited me. Buddhism had captured my heart, and I wanted to immerse myself in its teachings.

As I reached the top of the steps and paused to pose for a customary tourist snap, I could sense the eyes of the sacred statue on my back. Turning around, I was in awe at this beautiful piece of craftsmanship standing forty-five metres above me. It almost took my breath away (or was that the steps?). But what really got my attention that day was something inside the statue.

When you visit these sorts of tourist attractions, the thing that often lets them down is the commercial element – people profiteering from the huge lines of tourists ready to spend their hard-earned money on stuff they don't need. We had experienced this just a few days prior when visiting James Bond Island, in Phang Nga Bay, famous for being the place where *The Man With The Golden Gun* was filmed back in 1974. We had an incredible trip, don't get me wrong, but what I was expecting to find was an untouched island shimmering with all of Mother Nature's gifts; instead, what I found as we made our way around the island were endless market stalls full of 'tourist tat' which somehow seemed to dirty the purity of what should have been a beautiful and magical experience.

Visiting the Big Buddha was a unique experience for me altogether. It was completely free to visit – though donations were welcome – and despite the ongoing construction work happening around the perimeter, the grounds were relatively calm and free of people trying to barter with me for their goods. This brought me welcome relief. Moreover, as I stepped inside the entrance of this grand marble building, what I found instead of the expected market stalls were in fact rows of Thai Buddhist monks chanting and praying in their traditional orange robes. It was my idea of heaven.

As I waited patiently in the queue, I watched as one of the monks blessed each person and tied a customary multi-coloured bracelet around their wrist as a sign of their bless-ing. As I stepped forward for my turn, I held my breath and stood facing the monk. I locked eyes with him, determined he would hear my inner voice pleading with him, *please save my brother*. He bowed his head as if in acknowledgement of my prayer and tied a bracelet around my wrist. I didn't take it off for weeks following the trip, believing my prayer would be ruined if I removed it.

I recall becoming acutely aware in that moment of a sublime calmness washing over me and pulsating between me and every corner of the temple. I had found hope; I had found faith. Just as we were about to leave the temple, out of the corner of my eye I noticed a beautiful sand mandala laid out on the floor. I had never seen one before and was instantly curious about its meaning. Sand mandalas are used during Buddhist ceremonies as a reminder of the imperma-nence of life: that we are never in control, that life is always changing. Over several weeks, the mandala is constructed by monks using dense coloured sand. They usually start from the centre, working outwards. Mandalas differ in designs, but they're all complex in their structure and geometrical shapes. Once complete, a ritualistic ceremony is held for the complete destruction of the mandala. Upon learning this, I cringed inside. The idea of ruining such a beautiful piece of art that had taken weeks to create seemed wrong on so many levels – well, to my egoic mind, anyway. It was the same feeling I would get when watching sandcastles on the beach wash away as the tide rolled in. But something about this concept of impermanence struck a chord with me that day. I knew I needed to learn to become comfortable with the uncomfortable. It became a mission of sorts. I had been reminded by this simple ritual that it's in the resistance and discomfort that we must find our peace. It is futile to fight against the ever-changing nature of life. She's going to move anyway, so why not move with her?

THE ASHES

When you're told you're going to die, there are conversations that you and those closest to you simply cannot avoid. We sometimes have these same conversations even when we haven't been handed a terminal diagnosis, but they never seem to carry the heavy reality of being told death is right around the corner – you're next up. We somehow think death only comes to those who have been labelled with the word 'terminal'. Unfortunately, the majority of us wander around with blinkers on, still believing in the illusion of immortality, a form of make-believe. So when the curtain finally drops and reveals the Wizard hiding behind the veil, it suddenly becomes an entirely different conversation.

One of those difficult conversations centred around Syd's funeral and what to do with his remains. Never in my worst nightmares had I imagined that I would ever be having this conversation with my little brother. It seemed unfathomable. So, in a bid to do things differently, I spent many days trying to persuade him that my off-the-wall idea of having a funeral before he died wasn't so off-the-wall.

Syd was having none of it. 'You can't do that!' he pleaded.

He recoiled at the idea of other people speaking about him or making him the centre of attention in any way. He felt it would be embarrassing and would make him appear narcissistic somehow.

'But it's so pointless having everyone come and say all these wonderful things about you when you're not even there to hear it!' I exclaimed.

I was desperate for him to feel the love I knew everyone felt for him and to see what we all saw: that he was unique, special, and truly inspirational. I wanted him to die knowing what a difference he had made in other people's lives. He could never see what others saw in him – a problem so many of us have in life, I think. Of course, there are also those who suffer from the opposite (and often dangerous) affliction – those people who walk the earth thinking they are the centre of everyone's universe. Syd was most definitely not one of those people.

I had to accept that he wasn't going to agree to my magical '*This is your Life*' day. With folded arms and a big-sister sigh, I admitted defeat and moved the conversation on. We at least agreed on a venue and that it would be a celebration of his life, not a funeral. He wanted the opposite of morbid. He wanted joy, colour, and celebration – a party of sorts, in the place where our family had celebrated many birthdays, weddings and retirements, and the very place that had sponsored Syd when he raced his beloved Clio.

Then came the question of what would happen to his body. My stomach lurched at the thought. As I stared wide-eyed at the oil diffuser in the corner of the room which had been puffing away for hours, its plume of sweet-smelling vapour climbing and then disappearing into the ether, I imagined my brother's spirit as it might disappear the same way. As my heart skipped a beat, I took a deep breath and pushed the words out of my mouth.

'So, do you want to be buried or cremated?'

Despite my head wanting to sink down in despair at my question, I fought to keep it upright and kept eye contact with him the entire time. I wanted to show him I was going nowhere.

'Wow, what a question,' he said with his typical sarcastic tone.

'Well, we can't not talk about it. We don't have to dwell on it – we just need to know,' I said.

'Fine – cremated,' he replied. I noticed he stopped short as the conversation continued between me and my mum and dad. As we all chattered among ourselves, discussing possibilities for where his ashes might be scattered, I noticed out of the corner of my eye his brow furrowing and his head tipping to one side. He looked confused.

'What's up?' I asked.

'Why would you be talking about where to spread my ashes?'

I looked at him, puzzled. 'What do you mean?'

'I don't want you to scatter me anywhere – I want to stay with you, otherwise I'll be all alone.'

My heart melted and my eyes filled with tears. I took his hand, looked him square in the eyes, and said, 'You will never, ever be alone. I will always be with you, and you with me, remember?'

The problem with our egoic mind is that it convinces us we are separate from others, that we merely live in the physical world and that's all there is. But is it? I don't believe it is, and since Syd died, I have become increasingly sure of it.

For the two years following his death, I kept my promise, and those ashes sat on my mantlepiece alongside a photo of the two of us. And for those two years, I felt entirely uncomfortable. Something just wasn't sitting right with me. It was the same discomfort I had felt when watching his struggles in those final six months of his life – his fight to stay, his fight to resist and the subsequent knots he tied himself in. It felt to me like he was trapped in that box. And I was trapped with him. I was struggling to move forward, and I could sense he was too. I had this inner knowing that since his transformation he was laughing at his own request, realising how silly it was now that the illusion of separateness had been effectively shattered into smithereens. I knew it was time to ask him for a sign. I needed to know that he was thinking the same thing as me – and so I asked, and he answered almost immediately.

One day early in January 2021 I gently poured my morning cup of tea, taking it upstairs to bed. It was my favourite time of the day. As William Blake describes it, 'there is a moment in every day that the devil cannot find', and that was mine. Still thinking about the sign I had asked for from Syd, I reached over and picked up a book I had been reading – *Conscious Loving* by Gay and Kathlyn Hendricks. This was unrelated to my thoughts on Syd – in fact, it was quite the opposite: I had been reading the book to try to help me navigate the difficulties Rick and I were having at that time. It's a book, as it says on the front cover, to help couples find 'a way to be fully together without giving up yourself'. But as I turned the page that morning, it stopped me in my tracks. At the top of page 142, there were three words I will never forget: *Scattering the Ash*. I couldn't believe it. I gave a wry smile to myself; I had heard him loud and clear.

But it didn't end there. Two more signs came that very same day. I had not long since committed myself to reading *A Course in Miracles* – I would often find little gems of hope and comfort in the deep spiritual text – but it was absolutely not something I could tackle every day. Feeling Syd's energy, I picked it up and turned to a random page. As I opened it to page 105, this is what it said:

> *God did not make the body, because it is*
> *destructible, and therefore not of the Kingdom.*
> *The body is the symbol of what you think you are.*
> *It is clearly a separation device,*
> *and therefore does not exist.*

As I lay there in the semi-darkness of that midwinter's morning, I couldn't ignore the deep knowing I had that these signs were not a coincidence; they were coming from Syd. He was encouraging me to go through with my plan. In that moment, I made the decision that we were in this together. Something magical was happening, and I knew innately that this was part of both his healing and mine. By releasing his ashes, I could help set us both free.

I leant over and grabbed my phone from the bedside table. I wanted to check the calendar so I could make sure my diary was clear on 17th February. I would head over to Airton, where we grew up, and release his ashes into the river where we played as children at the exact same time he died – 3.40 p.m. As I swiped across to the seventeenth, I had to do a double-take for a moment. It was Ash Wednesday.

CHAPTER SEVENTEEN: FINDING ME

When the ego weeps for what it has lost, the spirit rejoices for what it has found.
Eckhart Tolle

As I begin the closing chapters of this book, it's tempting to draw some sort of grandiose conclusion – to present you with some sort of 'ta-da' moment, the final product, the perfect me. But for the first time in my life, I now know that there is no final destination, no finish line. As Marianne Williamson, American author, speaker, and political candidate, said, 'No one is ever finished. The top of one mountain is the bottom of another.'

Life, I am learning, is in fact a continual ebb and flow of joy, pain, and everything in between, and for the most part I am not in control. The only part I can control is who I am in the face of it all. And now I choose to be me. The truest, most authentic me.

The title of this chapter – 'Finding Me' – really should be 'Remembering Me' and everything I had forgotten. My answer to the age-old question 'What is the meaning of life?' is simply: to remember who we are. Everything we are looking for is already here, yet we spend an agonising number of years searching in all the wrong places. As Syd reminded me, I am the coat rack; I just had to get rid of the coats that didn't belong to me. Or, put in another way, as I once heard Eckhart Tolle say, 'You are the canvas, not the painting'.

As human beings, we have been given the gift of free will. If we don't like our painting, we can rub it out and start again. We don't have to accept the colours and textures that were painted on our canvas, either by us or by anyone else. It has taken time, but my paintbrush is firmly back in my hand, and I am no longer waiting for others to approve of my work. My painting is slowly beginning to reflect who I am and what I stand for, a creative expression of my raw, authentic self.

And just as in nature, my painting can and will change for every season of my life. The end of any season is always just the start of another. Another chance to create anew.

SO WHAT ARE YOU WAITING FOR?

In 2013, following Syd's fateful diagnosis, both he and I faced awkward reactions from others when the topic of his impending doom came up. He was always very upfront in his responses, which sometimes caught people off guard, but they would quickly realise that he was using humour and straight talking to help alleviate not only his own discomfort, but theirs.

It's always difficult to know what to say in these situations. We are often afraid of saying the wrong thing, causing more upset in an already unimaginable time in someone else's life – but underlying all of it, as I discussed in Chapter Thirteen, is our fear of talking about death. We prefer to continue living in denial, that make-believe world of immortality. We think we can just push it aside and worry about it when our time comes, or never face it at all.

The most common phrases we would hear from people would be things like 'I'm so sorry', 'It must be awful for you', 'I can't imagine what you're going through'. These words all came from a good place and were appreciated, but there was one phrase that would always frustrate Syd: 'He's so brave'. He would often comment to me through gritted teeth, 'I'm not brave – I just don't have a bloody choice.'

And I would wholeheartedly agree. He didn't want sympathy or an award for being the bravest – he found it patronising and total nonsense, because it seemed to indicate he was somehow different to everyone else, and he knew he wasn't. He knew that on the deepest, most fundamental level, we are all one, and we are all facing the same terminal diagnosis. What he really wanted most was for people to see life through the same lens he now did. He wanted to shake people and show them that they were fast asleep to life. He wanted people to see that from birth we are all handed a terminal diagnosis – we are all dying, and we need to wake up from our amnesic slumber and realise this profound truth before we reach an existential crisis of our own and realise that we have lived a life that was all wrong. This excerpt from Katherine Mannix's book *With the End in Mind* explains it beautifully,

Of course, it always seems that the best people are
dying. These are just ordinary people,
like the rest of us, but they are at an extraordinary
place in their life journey, and all of us benefit
from their compassion. They are not, in the main,
'saints'. They still have grumpy moments and
periods of intense sadness, fear, or anger about
their fate. But they are examples of what we can
all become: beacons of compassion,
living in the moment, looking backwards with
gratitude and forgiveness, and focused on the
simple things that really matter.

As Oliver Burkeman reminds us in his book *Four Thousand Weeks*, if we are lucky, we are gifted 4,000 weeks to live our one precious life. Syd had 1,850 (ish). Had he known this and faced the reality of his own mortality earlier in life – as we all should – and made different choices, perhaps things may have been different. No one will ever know. But what I do know is that we can either learn from those who have been taken too soon or we can ignore those lessons, stay asleep and keep repeating the same patterns.

As you read these words, perhaps now is the perfect time to reflect on the weeks you have already lived and how many more you may be gifted. Maybe you're unhappy in a relationship, maybe you can't stand your job, maybe you dream of running your own business, maybe you want to have children, maybe you want to live overseas . . . Just start where you are, get honest with yourself, and reflect on what is most important to you and only you. Try to understand what it is that's holding you back. Do the work. It's not easy, but it's the greatest gift you can give yourself. As J. Krishnamurti once said: 'To understand yourself is the beginning of wisdom'.

So what are you waiting for?

YOU HAD THE POWER ALL ALONG, MY DEAR

It was sometime in 2015.

As I lay on the bed with my eyes closed underneath a pillowy lavender eye mask, I took some deep breaths and listened attentively for my reiki teacher's soothing voice to begin. I had been looking forward to my guided meditation all week, and although comfortable with the growing spiritual world I was discovering around and within me, just like many people I still found myself cringing at times. I can remember one of my biggest cringe moments back then, and an area of exploration I would often avoid, was working on my 'inner child'. I couldn't even tell you now why that made me cringe so much; perhaps it conjured up thoughts of groups of hippies, sitting in a circle, holding hands, wailing and chanting. And having struggled throughout my teens and twenties to express myself fully, often shying away from anything that would make me look silly (I still battle with this now), I would resist venturing into this territory. I knew, though, that I had to keep pushing myself out of my comfort zone and embrace the cringe. So I listened carefully and allowed my thoughts to wander to a visualisation of my five-year old self.

And what I found on the other side of my discomfort was a place I could escape to in my mind that reunited me with little Kay— a safe space I could visit whenever I wanted, where I was able to sit with that little girl with the curly blonde hair and tell her everything was going to be OK. I could hold her hand and remind her of how special and how loved she was. I could reassure her that she was safe, and most importantly I could remind her that love was all around her, and fear was in fact just a concept she had learnt from others. I could show her that those fears were not real, and I could help her unlearn them.

As I practised these meditations more and more, I found that all of the cynicism I had about the concept of my 'inner child' would completely dissipate. I could finally see the true value of the process as I started to become aware of the self-compassion growing inside me. It would truly change my life and would, in the years to come, help me reconnect with Syd as our relationship transformed.

The synchronicity during that particular year was undeniable. As I discovered my inner child, in the very same year I was told it was all 'up to me' during that weekend in Melbourne. For the first time, I realised I had the power all along, just like Dorothy when Glinda the good witch said those famous words. But that was eight years ago, and as I've touched on throughout the book, we must be patient. Our yellow brick roads are long and winding, and we each have our own unique one to traverse. We will suffer setbacks along the way that may lead us down the wrong path, and it may take some time to find the right one. That's OK; it's all part of the journey. The key is to be honest with ourselves and find our way back. The truth is, as long as we sow the seeds of intention and nurture and care for those seeds, the flowers will eventually bloom. I recall writing my own seeds of intention in my hotel room during that weekend in Melbourne. I felt awake and alive in that moment, and I wanted to capture the feelings I was having to affirm how I wanted to see myself and my life ahead of me. I had the power. I could feel it in my bones.

I will listen to the impersonal me, the true me.
I won't make decisions out of fear. I will continue
to improve my ability to stay calm and at peace.
I will pursue my passions in life and encourage
others to do the same. I will not attach myself to
other people's opinions or worry what they may
think of me or the way I choose to live my life.
I will continue to improve on nurturing and
loving myself, in particular my body.
I will discard anything unnecessary from my
life and live simply. I will see the joy in even the
smallest of tasks and act with purpose.
I AM LIGHT.

HOME

What do you think of when you think of home? Is it a place? A person? A precious item? Or is it a feeling? Perhaps it's a mixture of all of those things?

When I was old enough to describe myself, I would often say I was a 'homebody'. For me, when I thought of home, I would think of the physical place where the people I loved lived. Four walls, a fireplace; warm, loving people inside; to my mind, it was as simple as that. Home was my safe place. As I grew older and began to realise that the physical home isn't always the safe place, the word 'home' began to take on different meanings. First, home became the people who made me feel safe; surely if I just spent time with them, no matter where we were, it would still always feel like home. But then I came to realise that people can be unpredictable – and they're not always safe, either. I would finally turn to Mother Nature, like my secret den, or the wishing pool along the river. Nature always felt like home – safe, grounding, ever changing, yet at its core somehow staying the same.

But as I continued to travel along the yellow brick road, I eventually found myself uncovering an even deeper truth. Home is not a place outside of me; it's a place inside of me that has been there all along. If I hadn't stepped out of the invisible cage, I would perhaps never have discovered this truth. It was about listening to the whispers of my true self – following my gut despite the discomfort. It became my commitment to my yoga practice, therapy, energetic healing, meditation, that 'cringy' inner child work, and submerging myself into those deep wells of repressed emotions. Through these practices, I knew I'd finally found a place where I could be at home with myself. A place where I felt free – at peace. No matter what was happening on the outside, this was a place inside of me that I could retreat to whenever I needed or wanted to. Just like my secret den as a child, a place no one else could touch. Let me take a moment to describe it to you.

Imagine a Narnia of sorts, a magical and enchanting forest: trees and beautiful, lush foliage as far as the eye can see. I can hear a small stream flowing, birds singing, and the humming of nature all around. As I place my hand on a wrought-iron gate covered in moss and leaves, it opens up like a portal to another realm. I look down and can see that I am a being of light – angelic, almost – no features as such, just golden and bright. Upon entering the forest, I am almost immediately greeted by another being of light. It looks just like me, but I can sense it's someone else. I know it's my little brother. We join hands and embrace. Beams of light shoot off and reverberate all around.

In this moment, I feel nothing but pure unconditional love, joy, comfort, and peace. We are out of the 'Truman Show' and into another world. We are together again – like peas and carrots.

I first imagined this place when I took part in the inner child session with my reiki teacher, a few years before Syd died. I was living in Australia, so it was my way of connecting from afar. Little did I know that Syd was visiting his own place around the same time. He wrote these words in 2017, which I wouldn't discover until after his death:

You ask yourself why I seclude myself here in my little forest hut? I just smile here and say nothing, listen to the quiet in my soul. This peacefulness lives in another world. That no one owns.

The synchronicity took my breath away. He was visualising the same place. How could this be? It only affirmed for me once again the power of the universal intelligence that surrounds us every minute of every day.

This visualisation practice has become one of my most treasured and valuable tools to use when facing any painful situation. And the beauty of it is I know I can access this place at any time. Meditation is a wonderful way to do it, but really, I can access it anywhere, any time: in the dentist's chair, the doctor's waiting room, during yoga, in the car, in the bath, when I'm sick in bed – there are no limitations. We get too hung up on looking for the perfect place to sit and meditate – we become too focused on the label of meditation and what it should look like. Ultimately, it should be designed by you, for you, and it only needs to make sense to you. That's all that matters.

I have come to understand that this place at the centre of my being is the place we are born from and the place we return to when we die. That 'quiet in the soul' Syd wrote about – that still point, the unmoved, the grounded, the rooted – it all circles back to this sense of home. When you look at the word 'home', you'll see it contains the word 'om'. The word 'om' – as defined in the Collins dictionary as 'a mystic syllable' – is a sacred mantra often referenced and used during meditation practices. It is said to be the sound of the universe, the primordial sound of creation. This sacred sound, which does not have reference to any religion or God, is nature in its purest form. We are, after all, vibrational beings, and from the first vibration, the sound of *om*, all other vibrations were able to come into being. This is the place I now call home. A place where I am safe, loved, and free. After Syd died, this place brought me a great deal of comfort. I could visit him whenever I needed to – our relationship became transformed from the physical to the spiritual.

I once heard a podcast in which the great author Elizabeth Gilbert was speaking candidly about her own journey following the loss of someone she loved deeply. She said, 'I can't live without her – so I don't.'

And *I* don't. An important part of my grieving process has been discovering how I don't have to leave Syd behind. I can move forward with my new life with him still by my side. He may no longer be physically here but, just like when we lived ten thousand miles apart, we have learnt to adapt to the circumstances, together.

Now I can see the deeper meaning of his last words here on earth:

'I want to go home.'

CHAPTER EIGHTEEN:
A PATHWAY TO INNER PEACE

*The person who has found inner peace can no
longer be intimidated, controlled, manipulated,
or programmed. In this state, one is invulnerable
to the threats of the world and therefore
has mastered life.*
David R. Hawkins

It's no secret that in our society today the vast majority of us
are feeling lost and disconnected – not only from each other
but, more worryingly, from ourselves. This isn't something
new. This has been happening since the beginning of time,
but it has never been known to happen on such a scale as it is
today. So what is driving this disconnection? Well, there are
many theories around this, and I don't know all the answers.
However, there is one aspect of our society that I believe is a
major driving force behind our general malaise, and that is
technology – or rather the misuse of technology, and more
specifically the internet.

Around thirty years ago we found ourselves waking up
to the dawn of a new era: the internet age. I was around ten
years old, and I can distinctly remember the buzz of excitement as we became 'connected' at school and in Dad's office,
and when our first computer landed right in the comfort of

our own home. Many people will recall the clunky sounds of their first dial-up modem, whirring and whistling as the computer attempted to connect. There's no doubt it was an exciting time for everyone; it was a time of progress and a time when we genuinely believed that the 'world wide web' would bring us closer together. How wrong we were.

Despite the excitement in the air, I can clearly recall glancing across at my mum as she uttered words that have stayed with me forever. As we unpacked and hoisted the huge white PC from its box, she said, 'I don't like the idea of this at all. It's going to be the end of us.'

Her comments at the time seemed so ridiculously dramatic. In fact I think we all creased over laughing and said something like, 'Yeah, whatever, Mum!' But there was something about what she said — the downright certainty in her voice, the conviction of her words — that stirred something inside of me. Maybe she was right?

It cannot be denied that the internet and technology more broadly have improved and enhanced our lives in the most incredible ways, but over time we have steadily become overloaded with information and yet completely starved of wisdom.

As with most things, the speed, awe and wonder of the internet have come at a price. Our health and wellbeing have been both directly and indirectly impacted in ways we have never seen before. We are feeling the effects on our mental and physical health, but worst of all we are spiritually the sickest we have ever been. The harsh reality is that we are addicted to our technology. Most of this addiction is fear-based, and no one is immune – no one. We are bombarded every minute of every day with advertising pop-ups, never-ending news feeds, hundreds of notifications, mindless content, emails at all times of the day and night, text messages, group chats . . . and all of it is driven by manipulative algorithms engineered by big tech companies to ensure your eyes are glued to your screen at all times. If you've seen the Netflix documentary *The Social Dilemma*, you will know exactly what I am talking about. If you haven't seen it, I would highly recommend it.

On a global scale, what we are really craving isn't our smartphones or devices; it's real, authentic human connection. We have made the mistake of thinking we are a problem that needs to be solved by the IT helpdesk, when in actual fact we're human beings crying out to be understood by one another.

We were not built to be 'switched on' twenty-four hours of the day; we were built for balance. As they used to say in the famous chocolate bar advert, we need to work, rest, and play – and not necessarily in that order. But instead, we're draining our life battery and never taking the time to recharge. Our mental bandwidth is currently choked with pings, clicks, likes, and shares. We have too many tabs open, and this leaves no room for the things that make us feel good. We have become dangerously distracted from what genuinely matters.

I recently heard someone describe this period we're living in as 'the quickening'. And I would have to agree that we are all moving too fast. And when we move too fast, what happens? Well, we begin to find that at this speed it's only possible to skim the surface of life, just like skimming a book; we get the general gist, but we miss the deeper meaning. What we are gaining in speed, we are lacking in substance, and as a result our souls feel hollow. We are becoming restless. We are innately aware that something's wrong, but we can't quite put our finger on what it is. We are desperately seeking something tangible, something real, something to hang on to, something that feeds our soul and lights us up from the inside out. We want to feel alive. So desperate are we to feel alive that we will behave in self-destructive ways in order to feel something– anything.

Isn't it ironic that we're more 'connected' than we have ever been in the history of humanity, yet our feelings of disconnect seem to plague us in every waking moment? The truth is, we are attempting to live in two worlds – effectively splitting ourselves in half– and it's not working for us. In fact, it's becoming so damaging that what we are seeing as a result is a rising obesity epidemic, disrupted sleep cycles, the worst levels of domestic abuse we have ever seen, a breakdown of the nuclear family unit– and all of this leading towards an increase in depression, anxiety, self-harm and a sharp rise in suicides, particularly in young people. No longer do we meet our friends in the park to talk; instead, we go to chat rooms online. We have stopped taking part in hobbies we used to love; instead, we sit on the couch, scrolling through our social media feeds. Our children are no longer playing games in the streets; they're stumbling around the living room with virtual-reality goggles glued to their faces for hours on end. And to make things worse, in 2020, as the pandemic hit, it was as if someone had pressed the boost button on *Sonic the Hedgehog* and the world was catapulted into a whole new level of disconnection. Our minds, bodies and spirits have been hijacked by big tech, and we are now living in a highly superficial, unnatural, digitised world. Remember what I said in Chapter Eight: we are not machines, yet we are living and working as if we are. Attempting to live this way leaves us feeling, as Ralph Waldo Emerson once said, 'disunited with ourselves'.

But I am here to tell you all is not lost. It's not all doom and gloom. It is possible to shift from a place of hopelessness to one of hopefulness – no matter what challenges we are facing in life. We have the power within ourselves to turn things around.

When I decided to write this book, I knew I wanted to help others. I wanted to be of service, but most of all I wanted to shine a light for those lost in the darkness, as others had done for me. But I could only do that if I walked the talk. I had to acknowledge that my Pollyanna attitude to life – trying to fix the world and everyone in it when I should have been looking inward – wasn't working for me any more. I've discovered that the best contribution we can make in this world is to master our self, and the rest will follow. But in order to do that, we must face our shadow selves. We have to be courageous and awaken our inner lion, and recognise that we are a direct reflection of the world around us. We are not just the yin; we are the yang, too. We are not just the perfectly posed photos on Instagram; we are the hot mess crying in the bathroom mirror feeling like our life is falling apart, too. We are all of it.

What we tend to dislike in others is often a projection of what we recognise within ourselves. It's not pretty, but in order to grow as people we must acknowledge this uncomfortable truth – and at the same time, we must remember that we are all the same and we're all just trying to do our best. We must stop berating ourselves and others and start where we are. There has to be acceptance of the situation we find ourselves in, and that has to come without blame. Blame – directed towards ourselves or others – is destructive, a form of cancer that can kill relationships and eventually its host. Blame will take aim at the heart and shoot fear-based emotions such as anger and guilt right at the centre. Nothing good has ever come from blame. It sits in the same category as worry: a pointless waste of our precious life energy. Once we have accepted our current circumstances (free from blame and judgement), then we are free to face our emotions. We grant ourselves the space to find healthier coping strategies, and eventually we are able to move forward and grow. No longer stagnant, resistant, and frustrated, we become free flowing.

In this closing chapter, I'd like to share with you **three pillars** that I developed and used as a guide on my own pathway to inner peace. Please feel free to change the word 'peace' to anything that aligns with you. It could be happiness, or freedom, or success, or contentment; whatever works for you, use that. The word doesn't matter, as long as it means something to you.

These three pillars I have titled **purpose**, **love**, and **faith**. They are based on the three essentials for happiness I discussed in Chapter Fourteen: **something to do**, **someone to love** and **something to hope for**. As I developed these pillars, I also drew upon the 'Wizard of Oz' analogy: the Scarecrow represents **purpose**, the Tin Man represents **love**, and the Lion represents **faith**.

Listed under each of these **three pillars** are **ten areas of focus** – things you may wish to consider and incorporate into your life. Some can be done immediately, while others may take more work, depending on where you are in your own personal journey of self-discovery.

As an extra resource, I have listed book recommendations at the back of the book so that you can delve in more detail into the areas you're most interested in, and I have included a shortened version of the pillars in a table format – an easy-to-use guide that you can refer to as regularly as you need to.

My wish for you, throughout this process, is to feel a strong sense of empowerment. To realise that you are in charge; you have all the answers; you are a sovereign being with the ability to navigate your way through life's difficulties.

As I write this, I am reminded of the words of William Ernest Henley's poem *Invictus*: 'I am the master of my fate;

I am the captain of my soul.' These words are a wonderful mantra to help remind ourselves that we are always in the driving seat. It's just that sometimes we fall asleep behind the wheel.

I also want to stress here that I am no expert, and that what I share with you is taken from my own experience. There is a great saying I once read – 'I don't want you to think like me; I just want you to think' – and it's true here. What I am offering is a guide, a framework for you to build on; the rest is entirely up to you. But what I can say for sure is that once I started to apply the three pillars and the corresponding areas of focus to my own life, I observed a significant shift in my energy levels, and I sensed the life force returning to my being. It was as if someone switched the lights back on. The narrow torchlight I had been living under suddenly burst into floodlights. I was no longer disconnected. I could sense a return to myself. So, take what you find useful and let go of the rest. Don't get bogged down in the detail, and initially perhaps select only one or two areas of focus from each pillar.

And of course, without action, they're just pretty words on a page. As the late, great Napoleon Hill details in his work on the principles of success, you need three things in order to be successful at anything in life: you must have a definite **purpose** and a clear **plan**, and you must **act**.

There are no shortcuts. If we want lasting change, we must do the work.

PURPOSE

Move Your Body

Express Yourself Creatively

Serve Others

Find Meaning and Purpose

Eat Real Food

Sleep Well

Hydrate

Minimise Toxicity in the Body

Take Supplements

Breathe

LOVE

Practise Forgiveness

Set Clear Boundaries

Keep a Journal

Process Repressed Emotions

Find What Feels Good

Love Consciously

Shrink Your Circle

Have a Digital Detox

Reframe Your Thoughts

Self-regulate

FAITH

Your Place in the Universe

Spend Time in Nature

Develop Rituals

Cultivate Wisdom

Pray

Meditate

Practise Gratitude

Trust Yourself

Read Spiritual Texts

Be Inspired

PURPOSE

MOVE YOUR BODY

It doesn't matter how, when, or where– just move it, daily. Take up a yoga class or a dance class, or perhaps kick-boxing is your thing? Take a daily walk, go for a workout at the local gym if that's your jam. Whatever you do, make sure it's well balanced (no extremes necessary) and make sure it's something that is easily accessible and that you enjoy, otherwise you will find it too difficult to stick to.

EXPRESS YOURSELF CREATIVELY

Ever wanted to take up a new hobby, or perhaps pick up an old hobby you let slide many years ago? Ever wanted to write poetry? Learn a new language? Perhaps you've always fancied picking up a paintbrush, but are too afraid of what others might think, or have always had a desire to do more gardening? Or do you love building Lego, or drawing land-scapes?

Whatever it is that's nagging at you, don't let it pass you by. In allowing your creative side to be expressed, you will feel lighter and more connected to yourself and the universe at large.

SERVE OTHERS

This could be anyone. The key here is that instead of asking yourself 'What's in it for me?' you should ask 'How can I serve?' You will find no matter whether it's family, friends, or a complete stranger, the more you serve, the more rewards you reap in return. I have found there is nothing more rewarding than being of service to others.

FIND MEANING AND PURPOSE IN YOUR WORK

If you hate your job, leave. You're not a tree. You're not stuck; you're just living with thoughts of lack and limitation. If you can't leave immediately, then make plans to leave. Just take that first step and put it out there to the universe that your intention is to change your direction, and suddenly you'll find opportunities will present themselves where you hadn't seen them before.

EAT REAL FOOD, NOT TOO MUCH, MOSTLY PLANTS

I take these words from Michael Pollan, an American author and journalist. I'm going to be brief here. When it comes to nutrition, it's all about being real and balanced. Ignore the fad diets and bring it back to basics. Eat foods that your body will recognise wherever possible. I'm still not a hundred per cent there, but I try to make good choices as often as possible. It's no good eating well if your thoughts about it are toxic; you'll only end up swallowing lashings of guilt, which can be more damaging than the food itself.

SLEEP WELL

The research has shown repeatedly that we should aim to get seven to nine hours' sleep every night. But let's not get too wrapped up in the numbers. The quantity is far less important than the quality. Some tips around good sleep hygiene include: creating a tech-free zone in the bedroom; not eating late at night (ideally not beyond 7 p.m.); and reducing or eliminating the use of alcohol or any other stimulants in the afternoon and evening. This is not an exhaustive list of dos and don'ts; they're just simple changes that I've found have helped me. Without a doubt, the most influential change for me was to eliminate alcohol from my life. Since then, I've slept soundly for seven to eight hours every night, and I wake up around the same time every day without an alarm.

HYDRATE

I have struggled with this one, because I've hated water most of my life. I don't ever remember drinking it as a child, and into adulthood I would avoid it. I find it boring and tasteless, and the only way I've been able to change my habits is to change the way I perceive it. If we don't water our plants, they wither and die. It's as simple as that. We have a basic need to hydrate to stay alive. I keep a litre bottle of water with me most of the day – it's the only way I remember to drink it. I often add fresh fruit to it to improve the taste.

MINIMISE TOXICITY IN THE BODY

We are exposed to toxicity every day; it's unavoidable. From toxins in the air that we breathe and the water we drink, all the way down to the clothes we wear, the skin-care and make-up products we lather over our bodies, and everything we ingest. It is impossible to eliminate all of these toxins; however, we can consciously reduce our exposure. Try to look for cleaner, natural options wherever possible, and reduce or eliminate toxic foods and drinks, particularly junk food and alcohol.

TAKE THE RELEVANT SUPPLEMENTS

There is no doubt that the food we ingest is no longer of the same quality it used to be; it is far removed from its natural form and therefore often depleted of essential vitamins and minerals. In addition, particularly in countries like the UK, we don't get enough vitamin D. This is an essential vitamin to ensure our immune system is well supported. There is a mountain of evidence to support the use of supplements, but there is also an equally large amount of information that seems conflicting. I am not a doctor or a medical professional, so seek out advice, whenever you're unsure – ideally from

from your doctor, pharmacist, functional medical doctor, homeopath, or integrative practitioner. And, most importantly, listen to your inner guidance when it comes to deciding what would benefit you and your body.

BREATHE

It sounds so simple, yet it's so powerful. Breathing wasn't something I ever thought about consciously until I started a regular yoga practice. Breathing deeply and consciously provides so many benefits to your overall health, it's astounding. I would highly recommend James Nestor's book on the subject called, simply enough, *Breath*. It's a real revelation.

LOVE

PRACTISE FORGIVENESS

I've covered this in Chapter Sixteen; however, I will say once again here that without forgiveness for yourself and others, you will stay stuck in a never-ending cycle of pain and suffering for the rest of your life. Now who wants that? Let it go. By practising forgiveness, you will deepen your relationships with those closest to you.

SET CLEAR BOUNDARIES

If you are someone who has never set boundaries, I'd suggest starting small and working your way up. You may be invited to a social event where you would normally (reluctantly) say yes to attending. Perhaps try saying no. Thank them for the invitation and express your appreciation that they thought of you, but express that you're unable to make it. Try not to follow up with a list of reasons to justify your 'no' – just stay confident in your ability to make a choice that is right for you.

KEEP A JOURNAL

Get the thoughts out of your head and onto the paper. You never need to show anyone the words you've written, so there's no pressure for this to be anything other than a way of moving thoughts out of your cells and onto the page. Another benefit of the practice of journaling is that it can be used as a way to reflect back and identify any negative patterns that arise in your life – this will help you focus on the areas of your life that need extra work.

PROCESS REPRESSED EMOTIONS

If you are having difficulties in your relationships, or you are wanting to embark on deep emotional processing, then therapy of some kind could be a good strategy. There are lots of therapies available out there that can support you. I have found that by trying a variety, I've been able to narrow it down to the therapies that suit me the most. Therapy doesn't start and end with a psychotherapist or a counsellor. There are plenty of other therapies out there, such as cognitive behavioural therapy (CBT), Emotional Freedom Technique (EFT), the Internal Family Systems Model (IFS), acupuncture, reiki, massage, reflexology, sound therapy, and many more. Always consult a healthcare professional when you are considering any therapy– preferably someone who focuses on the 'whole person'.

FIND WHAT FEELS GOOD

The American yoga instructor Adriene Mischler, who runs the programme *Yoga with Adriene*, uses the phrase 'find what feels good' throughout her videos (which you can find on YouTube or via her subscription service of the same name). I love this phrase. I repeat it to myself often. It helps me when making decisions. *Will this make me feel good?* If it won't, I will generally avoid it.

LOVE CONSCIOUSLY

In all relationships, it's important to keep your heart open. The minute we close off and love from a place of fear, we are no longer loving consciously. We have gone back to sleep, and we end up back in the blame cycle. It's difficult to keep our hearts open during tough times, yet this is when we most need to do it. To love consciously is to be completely vulnerable with your partner, opening up and being able to share all parts of yourself without judgement, accepting that each of you is a work in progress. For me, a consciously loving relationship is one where you are both deeply committed to your own and each other's personal growth.

SHRINK YOUR CIRCLE

I think we can all agree that it's important to have friends and family in our lives– and I'm not talking about Facebook friends. What truly matters is the quality of the relationships we surround ourselves with; two genuinely close connections are worth more than twenty superficial ones. It sounds ruthless, but in order to protect your inner peace, you must weed out the negative influences in your life– and that probably includes some of the people you surround yourself with.

HAVE A DIGITAL DETOX

Recently I decided to take a digital detox. In similar circumstances to when I removed alcohol from my life, I had this nagging inner voice telling me it was damaging to my health. My overly sensitive nature was overwhelmed by the daily exposure to everybody else's existence. I was intrigued to know whether it was contributing to my general feelings of anxiety and overwhelm, so I took the plunge and removed my profile from all social media platforms for a period of three months. There is no doubt that this hiatus has positively impacted my life on so many levels. I feel freer, lighter, and more focused than ever before. It's the reason I have been able to finish this book. As Robin Sharma said in his book *The 5AM Club*, 'we need to stop managing our time, and start managing our focus'. It was quite an eye-opener realising how much of my time had been wasted scrolling through meaningless content. We are all blessed with the same twenty-four hours in a day; we must choose wisely how we use those hours. When you're unsure, ask yourself: how would you like to see your child spend those hours? I bet your answer isn't for them to spend it all on their smartphone or tablet– so why are you any different?

REFRAME YOUR THOUGHTS

Buddha said 'what you think, you become', and I have found this to be true. It's often not the circumstances of your life that you are struggling with; it's your thoughts about it. Learning to reframe my own negative thought patterns helped me to overcome the traumatic events of Syd's death day by enabling me to see those past events through fresh eyes. With regular practice, I am no longer stuck in those negative thought patterns, and I've been able to overhaul old belief systems that were no longer serving me and had plagued me since I was a child.

SELF-REGULATE

We spend a lot of time during our lives relying on those closest to us to bring us happiness. Our expectations of others are unrealistic and at times downright unfair. We are grown adults, and our lives are our own responsibility – no one is going to live them for us. In order to break away from this reliance on others to *fix* us, we must learn to self-regulate. There are many tools available, but simple breathing practices are easily accessible and highly effective; I have also found a practice called Emotional Freedom Technique (EFT, also known as 'tapping') to be incredibly effective, particularly for an acute episode of anxiety. And the beauty is that it can be used any time, anywhere. Yoga and meditation have also been life-changing for me. No matter what emotion I am experiencing, I can be sure that these practices will ease the pain and allow me to manage most situations.

FAITH

BE AWARE OF YOUR PLACE IN THE UNIVERSE

When our lives seem unbearable, sometimes all we need is to take a step back, pause and marvel at the fact that despite our troubles, we are here, standing on a spinning rock in the vastness of an infinite universe . . . so does that parking ticket really matter?

Worrying about anything, I have learnt, is futile. When has worry ever changed the outcome? We don't get to call the shots. We are a mere speck of stardust, existing within a tapestry of interconnected energy and floating in what Deepak Chopra calls a 'quantum soup'. (Deepak Chopra, *The Spontaneous Fulfillment of Desire: Harnessing the Infinite Power of Coincidence*). We are all one, all connected at the deepest level, gracing the earth for just a short period of time. So don't sweat the small stuff.

In order to appreciate this universal awareness, try to make a habit of practising moments of awe: anything that will take your breath away, like the stunning view from a mountaintop, stargazing in a velvety night sky, or marvelling at a beautiful sunset displaying colours across the sky that no man could ever replicate. Whatever works for you, do that.

SPEND TIME IN NATURE

I'm a volunteer at the local hospice, and it's perhaps the most rewarding work I have ever done in my life. Recently I worked with a group of young children (around nine years old) who had been through a significant change or had experienced the loss of a close family member; this was often the death of a parent or grandparent, but in one child's case his family had fled the war in Ukraine to safety in the UK.

During one of our sessions together, the children were encouraged to talk about their feelings and how they make themselves feel better when experiencing difficult feelings like sadness or anger. I was astounded at how many of the responses related to nature. One child talked about being with horses and how she couldn't explain why, but they always made her feel better. Another talked about his chickens and how cuddling them eased his sadness. And another talked about being with their pet dog and how this would instantly dilute the pain they felt. I learnt that day that children are wise. They have the ability to self-soothe even when they don't have the language to explain it. In many ways, children are a blank canvas, with no preconceived views of how the world is or should be. They often 'find what feels good' without being prompted. They don't make decisions with their head; they will let their heart take the lead.

DEVELOP RITUALS

Rituals are an important part of life and are a recognised practice around the world in all cultures. They may help us mark a particular moment— the beginning or ending of a chapter in our lives, the death of a loved one, an important milestone— or can simply be a way to encourage self-discipline, like lighting a candle before working on a project, or making a cup of tea before your morning workout. Think about introducing rituals into your life where you feel you need to process or practise letting go of that which no longer serves you. As part of my practice to deepen my connection to nature, I follow simple rituals to mark the seasons throughout the year. Remember, these rituals don't need to be grand gestures; they can be something as simple as lighting a candle and repeating an affirmation or mantra, or a quiet prayer.

Why are rituals important? Well, one of the most well-recognised rituals in the world is that of a funeral, where we come together with family and friends to express our collective grief following the death of a loved one. What would happen if we skipped this ritual? Or what would happen, for example, if we didn't allow a child to attend? As many people have experienced in recent years, the impact of a global pandemic meant restrictions in the numbers of people attending funerals. It's a complex subject, and an entire book could be written about the harm caused to both children and adults alike by missing this important ritual. But, in short: when we are unable to express our grief through the ritual of a funeral, we are failing to honour the feelings that need to be moved and shifted from our mind, body, and soul, allowing us to move on through the next phase of the grieving process.

It has been well recognised and documented that in order to process our grief, there are a number of tasks we must take part in. The American psychologist J. William Worden developed these four tasks of mourning to help direct the pathway to growth beyond grief. The first task is that we **accept the reality of the loss**; the second task is that we must **process the pain of grief**; thirdly, we begin to learn new ways to **adjust to a world without our loved one**; and finally, in the fourth task, we **find an enduring connection with the deceased while embarking on a new life**. These tasks have been linked to the seasons in nature here on earth: autumn, winter, spring, and summer, in that order.

The ritual of a funeral sits within the first two tasks and plays a pivotal role in this process. Without it, both children and adults alike can find themselves stuck in the winter of grief for extended periods of time, unable to move forward. I have seen and heard many stories of children who have missed out on attending the funeral of a loved one because their family believed it was better to protect them from the sadness and pain, but the outcome of this is almost always that the child is left with feelings of anger, resentment and confusion that can in turn lead to struggles in adulthood with emotional regulation, challenges in relationships and often a reliance on unhealthy coping mechanisms to survive the pain of their repressed emotions. Being honest with children about death may be difficult, but it's essential if we are to support their emotional wellbeing.

CULTIVATE WISDOM

Apart from a rare few people – the 'old souls' of the world – we are not born with wisdom. Nor does wisdom just fall into our lap; we have to cultivate it for ourselves. In order to do this throughout our lives, we must have, as Wayne Dyer would say, 'a mind open to everything and attached to nothing'. We have to stay curious about life. Turn off the TV and pick up a book, talk to your elderly relatives, listen to children, open yourself up to learning new things, talk to people with opinions that are different from yours, and most important of all: get to know yourself. The problem we have is the constant tidal wave of information being thrown at us on a daily basis, with very little wisdom attached. In order to cultivate real wisdom, we must cull the noise and tune in to a higher frequency.

PRAY

Have you ever prayed for something? Maybe when you were a child you closed your eyes and prayed that Father Christmas would bring you that fancy new bike, the one you'd been dreaming of all year. Or maybe as an adult you prayed you would win the lottery so you could leave your hideous job, or that it would stop raining so your birthday party wouldn't be ruined this weekend? I think we have all prayed for things that seemed important – but are they really what we should be praying for? And perhaps the fact that these prayers often go unanswered means we are likely doing it wrong.

To pray, in its simplest form, is to commune with God. But let me remind you again here that this is not based on religion. Please change the word 'God' to whatever feels most comfortable to you. It could be the universe, nature, higher self, source, spirit or even Louise! What you call it is irrelevant, as long as it works for you. Making prayer a regular part of your 'something to hope for' practice can help to strengthen your faith that something bigger than you is taking care of things. It can help relieve you of anxiety and bring calm when you are going through a turbulent time in your life. It can remind you that everything is as it should be and that all is being taken care of all the time, no matter what you do.

Does this mean getting on your knees to pray every night before bed? Absolutely not. A prayer can be silent or loud, big, or small; it can be done anywhere, at any time. The key is that it must have true meaning and be in alignment with your higher purpose.

In May 2020, during the worst years of my life, I prayed. I prayed in a way I have never prayed before. I was sitting outside in the garden, reading. I was alone. It was during lockdown, and Rick and the boys were in the house. I had been living through a nightmare, watching my husband crumble under the weight of mental torment while trying to tackle my own never-ending grief. Since his surgery that went wrong the previous year, he had been living with a temporary stoma, meaning he was no longer able to go to the toilet and had to change his stoma bag instead. Ordinarily, this is a relatively straightforward process; having witnessed hundreds of patients living with a stoma, I know it's something many people are able to live with relatively well. Rick unfortunately had complications that none of us expected. Within a few months of his surgery, we noticed an area of his stomach which began to protrude forward slowly, putting pressure behind his stoma. We later discovered it was a football-sized hernia pushing out directly behind his stoma. This resulted in his stoma being pushed flat, meaning he was unable to get his stoma bag to stay in place. It leaked constantly. This meant he was often afraid to leave the house in case it leaked in public, which it did on several occasions – once on a train journey, and several times in bed – which left him incredibly upset, embarrassed and ashamed. It didn't matter what I did or said; I just couldn't comfort him during this time. It was torturous, and I felt helpless; we both did. Understandably, his unhealthy coping mechanisms and addictions ramped up over this period, and his mental state was the worst I had ever witnessed. He was suicidal and I felt I was losing him.

In a desperate bid to save his life that day, out of total desperation, I prayed. I had nothing left, so I turned to something bigger than me to help. It was the first time in my life I didn't feel stupid or self-conscious about it. I knew that in that moment I was connected to a universal intelligence. I knew what I was asking for was in alignment with my true self. There was no ego attached. I put my book down at my side, closed my eyes to the afternoon sun, and prayed in a way I had never done before. I asked Syd for help. And I asked with complete conviction – no messing. I meant every word, from the depths of my being. Rick needed reversal surgery urgently, but due to the pandemic halting all non-emergency surgeries, he wasn't classed as a priority. What I was asking for was a miracle.

I woke up the next day to the postman arriving. I heard Rick rush to the door, and then the sighs of disappointment that followed as he realised the letter he was so desperately waiting for hadn't materialised yet again. Then, later that afternoon, his phone rang. I watched as he left the room to take the call upstairs. Something arose inside me. I knew this was it: the answer to my prayer. After he failed to come downstairs for what felt like an eternity, I ran two steps at a time and pushed open the door of the spare room. He looked up at me with tears in his eyes and said, 'It was the hospital. I've got a date.' I swung my arms around him, buried my head in his neck, and wept.

MEDITATE

I have heard it said that if prayer is us talking to God, then meditation is where we receive the answer. I like this idea.

Meditation has been practised for hundreds of years across a variety of religious traditions, most notably Buddhism and Hinduism, with its earliest records found in the *Upanishads*, the ancient Sanskrit texts of the East.

When we talk about meditation, the first thing that often comes to mind is a vision of a calm, serene, traditional Buddhist monk sitting in a monastery in the middle of Nepal. It's a vision that's so far from our reality in the West and often so unrelatable that many of us fail to see how this practice could be incorporated into our everyday lives – a valid point. The problem is that we're often more concerned about how this practice looks to others, rather than focusing on its transformative benefits. We get too hung up on when, how, and where we will practise meditation, how long should we do it for, how we should sit, what time of day it should be . . .

We end up lost and it all seems too hard, so we don't bother.

I have tried and failed at a variety of meditation practices. But the trick, I have found, is to just keep trying. Eventually, something will stick. It's only recently that I have found my groove and been able to practise semi-regularly – certainly more regularly than I ever have before. And as with anything, once you start seeing the positive results, it's easier to stick to. For me, it's no longer a chore but something I look forward to. I feel calmer and more peaceful, and it has helped to slow down my overthinking mind.

I will share my current practice here, which may help inspire you to give it a go.

I practise for ten minutes, no longer; any longer, and I won't stick to it. I practise as soon as I finish my yoga practice, because this way I find my mind is already primed and 'in the zone'. I usually lie down in a yoga asana pose that encourages my body to relax and open, such as *baddha konasana*. I find it helpful to use pillows, a bolster, a weighted eye mask and some calming music. To hold my focus, I use either an affirmation which I repeat in silence or a breath practice to relax my mind. When thoughts do come in, I have learnt through practice not to fight with them, but instead to acknowledge them, observe them and allow them to pass through, then bring my focus back to my breath.

If you're finding it difficult to take the time out, maybe it's time to make a change to your schedule. We can all find ten minutes in our day. If you can't, then find five minutes, or two. Or maybe stop calling it meditation. Again, I think labels hold us back. By labelling something, we can build it up too much in our heads, instead of just getting on with it.

PRACTISE GRATITUDE

Are you an optimist or a pessimist? Do you surround yourself with positive or negative people? When you meet with other people, do you tend to fall into the habit of talking about your woes, sorrows, and the terrible weather we are having? No one wants to be a 'negative Nancy' or a joy thief, do they? Yet we meet them every day – hell, I have been one on many occasions, and I have definitely lived with them. The problem is that when you look for yellow cars, then suddenly that's all you see; the red cars seem to disappear. But they haven't, have they? They're always there – you've just put your attention elsewhere. The same applies to life. If all you look for is ugliness, then that is all you'll find. It works in exactly the same way for beauty. What does this have to do with practising gratitude? Well, when we practise gratitude, we are training our minds to focus on all that we are grateful for, all the beauty in our lives. And what we focus on, we attract. It's the law of attraction.

To practise gratitude, start simply by taking a small notebook and writing down three things you are grateful for each day. For example, you may be grateful for a lunch date with a friend, someone holding a door open for you, a warm cup of tea made by your partner – it doesn't have to be something grand. It's often the simplest things that make the biggest difference. You will find over time that you no longer need to write them down, because they will just come naturally to you; you will become grateful for so many things and see beauty everywhere.

TRUST YOURSELF

How many times have you said to yourself 'I should have listened to my gut'? How many times have you kicked yourself, knowing you were right all along but made a decision that was heavily influenced by others? You buckled under the pressure. It's happened to the best of us. In many ways we have stopped trusting ourselves. We have handed our power to other people.

When the four of us moved to Australia all those years ago, I was terrified at the idea of being alone, without our family or friends for support. I would lament how nothing would ever be the same, and felt discouraged at the thought of how we would 'do life' without their input. Well, after ten years alone, I had no idea just what a revelation it would be. Suddenly, for the first time in my life, I could make decisions without any interference from anyone else– nobody's opinions, or judgements, or unwelcome advice. I felt a freedom I had never felt before. I began to trust my own judgement and felt more empowered as the years went on. I decided I no longer wanted to sing from the same hymn sheet as everyone else; I wanted to write my own song. It was scary, but it was entirely liberating. When we returned to the UK in 2017, that noise descended once again – fiercely. After the initial shock – it felt like learning a new language again – I found new ways to shut out the noise. I created some boundaries and was able to trust in myself once more.

I want to add here that I'm not saying you should never take advice or listen to anyone else. What I am saying is: trust yourself first and foremost, then if you are still struggling, seek answers from those you can trust.

READ SPIRITUAL TEXTS

In trying to cultivate wisdom, I have found that many of the seeds of knowledge come from ancient spiritual texts. When we are seeking guidance, looking for answers, and we have run out of options – for example, if we're experiencing a 'dark night of the soul' – spiritual texts have the power to bring great comfort and solace. They can spark something deep inside of us, reminding us that in every moment we are supported by a higher power. Some people take comfort in the Holy Bible, some the *Bhagavad Gita*, others the Tao. Whatever your choice, seek out the one that resonates the most deeply with you, and allow it to cleanse your soul.

BE INSPIRED

We all need inspiration when we're feeling flat. When our life energy is low, we need to recharge and get back 'in spirit'. And it can be difficult to feel inspired in a world that seems to have lost its way. But in all of the centuries gone by, the world has never been free of war, environmental disaster, poverty, greed, or humanity's never-ending need for power over all. It's all an illusion, of course, that we might find ourselves in the worst century of all. So what can we do to feel inspired?

If you take the time to look, you will find inspiration in many places. There are a number of things I try when I feel flat and deflated. I will go for a walk, listen to podcasts, read a book, take a trip to the cinema or just be near the ocean. The goal is the same: I have to get out of my head or out of my body, leaving space for inspiration to enter my soul.

FINAL THOUGHTS

I miss my little brother. I will always miss the physical version of Syd. There is no doubt about it: the grief will never leave me. I know I will never 'get over it', but I have learnt to grow through and around it, and my life has become bigger than the grief. There will always be moments when I am pulled back into my grief – I have found this can happen without warning – but I now embrace those moments, seeing them as a reminder of how big our love was and still is.

The added complication of trauma made my journey more difficult, for sure. But with the right support, healing practices, and determination to no longer live in constant pain, I have learnt to embrace my new life and no longer be defined by my old sleepy one. Moving beyond Syd's death day has been my biggest challenge in life, but I'm now at a place where those events no longer dictate or rule my existence. The guilt that plagued me for not being able to stop the events of that day almost ruined my life. Had I continued to deny and run away from those feelings, I would not be writing these words today. I know I will never be able to change what happened, but there is something that tragic day can never take away from me, and that is my ability to choose how I react to it. I am slowly becoming the master of my own thoughts. That is where my power is.

As I write these words today, I am forty-three years old; I am a wife, a mother, a sister, a daughter, a friend, a writer, a counselling student, and a business owner. But most important of all, I am a student of life. I am no longer defined by titles, and I know that no matter what life throws my way, I have two choices: I can either resist or I can let it go.

On paper, my life is in many ways a disaster, yet on the inside I am the happiest and most at peace I have ever been. How has this been possible? Because I have shifted from trying to beat life to learning to flow with life. I've stopped competing, I've put my boxing gloves down, and I've begun collaborating. I've stopped resisting and I now let life pass through and around me. I'm learning to embrace all of it, choosing how I react; no longer pushing and striving for perfection, instead celebrating all of life's imperfections.

I used to dread getting old. During my twenties and thirties, I fell into the trap of chasing endless youth, but I no longer subscribe to that attitude. Every chapter of life is beautiful – don't be fooled into thinking otherwise. How boring it would be to live a life trapped in youth. I see every day, month, and year of my life as another opportunity to create and craft a life I do not wish to escape from – another chance to choose who I want to be and how I want to show up.

I realise now that everything we have ever needed to live a life of peace and happiness has always been available to us; we've just become unknowingly trapped in the invisible cage, distracted by the 'Truman Show' and struggling to see the wood for the trees. I've realised that heaven isn't some dreamy place in the sky, some utopia we go to when we die – it's been right here on earth all along, inside each and every one of us, like a glittering piece of gold waiting to be mined.

This would have been Syd's fortieth year, had he stayed. But his soul journey meant he had other places to be. I am now at peace with that. I feel honoured to continue traversing the universe alongside him, knowing that we are connected forever, no matter where we are.

He was here.

I am here.

ACKNOWLEDGEMENTS

Writing a book has been one of the hardest, yet most rewarding things I have ever done. Hours quickly turn into days, days turn into weeks , and eventually weeks turn into years. It 's an experience like no other, and although lonely at times, there are people that have played an integral part in the birth of this book. I want to take this opportunity now to express my sincere gratitude for those people who made sure I never gave up.

Tony, my mentor, and friend. Thank you for the endless coffee dates and book chat. Your advice has been invaluable. This book would never have existed had it not been for your faith in me and my ideas.

To all at 2QT Publishing – thank you for bringing the book to life. Special thanks to Catherine - from our very first meeting I knew from your gentle, authentic approach that you would ensure that the finished result would honour my brother and I. Thank you for your guidance.

To my soul tribe – Shanelle, Ming, and Jeanette – thank you for your unconditional love and countless hours of un-paid therapy throughout this process. You will forever be my soul sisters. I love you all deeply.

To my Mum and Dad. Your love, guidance, and inspiration to continuously extend myself has strengthened my will and determination to carry on no matter what circumstances are thrown my way.

To my boys, Louis, and Taylor – thank you for always believing in me. You have never failed in reminding me of what matters most. You truly light me up.

And finally, to the most important man in my life. My soulmate, Rick. Without you, I would still be that little crab under her rock hiding from the world. Thank you darling for teaching me how to be brave. Your love and unwavering support for *all* of me, on the good days and the bad, has kept me going on this crazy journey. I love you - always and forever.

BOOK RECOMMENDATIONS

1. *The Untethered Soul: The Journey Beyond Yourself* by Michael Singer. Published by New Harbinger Publications

2. *Cured: The Power of Our Immune System and the Mind-Body Connection* by Jeff Rediger. Published by Penguin

3. *Wintering: The Power of Rest and Retreat in Difficult Times* by Katherine May. Published by Riverhead Books.

4. *Eastern Body, Western Mind: Psychology and the Chakra System as a Path to the Self* by Anodea Judith. Published by Clarkson Potter/Ten Speed.

5. *Finding Meaning: The Sixth Stage of Grief* by David Kessler. Published by Scribner.

6. *Four Thousand Weeks: Time Management for Mortals* by Oliver Burkeman. Published by Farrar, Straus, and Giroux.

7. *A Radical Awakening: Turn Pain into Power, Embrace Your Truth, Live Free* by Shefali Tsabary. Published by HarperOne.

8. *Be More Human: How to transform your lifestyle for optimum health, happiness, and vitality* by Tony Riddle. Published by Penguin Life.

9. *Dying to Be Me: My Journey from Cancer, to Near Death, to True Healing* by Anita Moorjani. Published by Hay House.

10. *Radical Remission: Surviving Cancer Against All Odds* by Kelly A. Turner. Published by HarperOne.

11. *Radical Hope: 10 Key Healing Factors from Exceptional*

Survivors of Cancer & Other Diseases by Kelly A. Turner. Published by Hay House Inc.

12. *Yoga and the Quest for the True Self* by Stephen Cope. Published by Bantam.

13. *Inner Engineering: A Yogi's Guide to Joy* by Sadghuru. Published by Harmony.

14. *The Power of Intention: Learning to Co-create Your World Your Way* by Wayne W. Dyer. Published by Hay House Inc.

15. *Change Your Thoughts – Change Your Life* by Wayne W. Dyer. Published by Hay House Inc.

16. *When the Body Says No: The Cost of Hidden Stress* by Gabor Mate. Published by Vintage Canada.

17. *Quit Like a Woman: The Radical Choice to Not Drink in a Culture Obsessed with Alcohol* by Holly Whitaker. Published by The Dial Press.

18. *This Naked Mind: Control Alcohol, Find Freedom, Discover Happiness & Change Your Life* by Annie Grace. Published by ASPN Publications.

19. *Letting Go: The Pathway to Surrender* by David R. Hawkins. Published by Veritas Publishing.

20. *With the End in Mind: Dying, Death, and Wisdom in an Age of Denial* by Kathryn Mannix. Published by Little, Brown Spark.

21. *Conscious Loving: The Journey to Co-Commitment* by Gay Hendricks. Published by Bantam.

22. *The Seat of the Soul* by Gary Zukav. Published by Simon & Schuster.

23. *Stolen Focus: Why You Can't Pay Attention – and How to Think Deeply Again* by Johann Hari. Published by Crown.

24. *Big Magic: Creative Living Beyond Fear* by Elizabeth Gilbert. Published by Riverhead Books.

25. *Untamed* by Glennon Doyle. Published by The Dial Press.

26. *The Four Agreements* by Miguel Ruiz. Published by Amber-Allen Publishing.

27. *Daring Greatly: How the Courage to Be Vulnerable Transforms the Way We Live, Love, Parent and Lead* by Brene Brown. Published by Avery.

28. *Breath: The New Science of a Lost Art* by James Nestor. Published by Riverhead Books.

29. *Judgement Detox: Release the Beliefs That Hold You Back from Living a Better Life* by Gabrielle Bernstein. Published by Hay House UK Ltd.

30. *The Ecology of the Soul: A Manual of Peace, Power, and Personal growth for Real People in the Real World* by Aidan Walker. Published by O-Books.

ABOUT THE AUTHOR

Kay Backhouse was raised in the Yorkshire Dales, a picturesque part of the UK. It was here where she developed a strong connection to, and an appreciation for nature and it's healing properties.

At the age of twenty-eight she emigrated to Australia where she lived with husband, Rick and their children for ten years.

Kay now lives with her family in the coastal town of Morecambe in Lancashire. Through her writing, yoga practise and hospice work, she spends most days working with adults and children, helping them to navigate their way through grief and significant loss. She truly believes that we have the potential to overcome any adversity and that the power to achieve this lies inside each and every one of us.

Milton Keynes UK
Ingram Content Group UK Ltd.
UKHW041849090224
437493UK00001B/1

9 781914 083938